SEEK A CITY SAINT

Holiness is quaint—
Look at Holy Joe.
Seek a city saint—
Is he nice to know?

'Worldliness is sin,'
Rocker said to Mod.
Dig the city's din—
Find a holy God.

SEEK A CITY SAINT

DAVID HEAD

THE MACMILLAN COMPANY

New York

First American edition 1965

The Macmillan Company, New York

Library of Congress catalog card number: 65–17312

Printed in the United States of America

dedicated
without permission
but with gratitude and love
to our dear 'Auntie Matthews'
whose doctor called her a saint
and who is so very
'nice to know'

Contents

Holy Worldliness

'godliness in the present age'

1

Ash Wednesday

Dear Joe,

Holy worldliness! You have, you tell me, found those two words walking arm in arm through the pages of a book or two you have picked up recently. I agree that you would not have expected them to enjoy one another's company. As different as chalk and cheese—one white, one maggoty! As immiscible as oil and water, though the attempt might produce some bright colours! We have it on St Jude's authority that archangels rebuke devils, not sit down to tea with them.

You tell me that your self-appointed discipline this Lent is to live in earshot of the discord of those two words, and that you would like me to produce the music. This is not 'giving something up' for Lent, but taking something on. Where will it lead? Presumably to Good Friday and Easter. A death and a resurrection? Perhaps that is what is needed to make sense and solidity out of 'holy worldliness'.

Most of your letter was about holiness. What, you ask, does holiness mean for an ordinary Christian in city life today? Knowing you as a genuine sort of person just settled in a large city after some years at sea, I am sure

you are asking the right question. I am not so sure that
you are asking the right person.

The more I try to get hold of the meaning of holiness
—and it takes a strong grip—the more a voice inside me
shouts 'Not for me', while another voice quietly insists,
'Yes, all of it'. If I did not hope that there were traces
of it in my life, I could not write to you at all. Even
though our words keep well ahead of our lives, none of
us has the right to say, 'Now don't look at me, but listen
to what I say.' St Paul did not hesitate to say outright,
'Copy me', or when he had more time to express himself,
'Copy me, as I copy Him'. This sounds terrifying, but
I must credit you with the sense to look beyond my
example to my Example. I am beginning to realize
how little I think about holy living. Is that because I am
afraid of becoming self-consciously pious or morbid or
proud about it? Or because, having rejected the tonsure,
I want to avoid the lunatic fringe? Or because the price
is too high?

You ask what holiness means for the 'ordinary Christian'.
You must realize that ordination changes a man's way of
life, and changes a man. There is a professionalism which
is apparently unavoidable, whether for doctor, teacher
solicitor, or minister of religion. Each one of them takes
it as a compliment if someone fails to spot their occupation
from their manner. Some clergy manage to go to
extremes. So I must warn you that a minister writes
from a life with many a clerical plus, such as theological
training and easy contact with people, and many a
clerical minus, such as the effect of a thousand hand-
shakes and the lack of the discipline of a five-day-week
routine. But, come to think of it, most of my work is
among laymen; and I was one myself.

As for my knowledge of 'city life today', I have never

supposed that there is a conspiracy among those who are at the college-end of our training or the pew-end of our ministries, to impose an other-worldly brain-wash and body-polish. Yet college days and local church life can make us remote from the ways of people 'in the world'.

We ministers need the determined help of lay people like yourself, to provide the strong line to prevent our being swept away from firm life-as-it-is-lived by the sucking currents of ecclesiastical chores. I cannot pretend to have escaped the undertow, and I shall keep on warning you that it can easily happen to 'ordinary Christians' as well.

Yet the daily contacts and the television set and the proximity of thieves and neighbours (not to be confused) and the local politics and the rush-hour roads, all of which we share with everyone else, will continually remind us that any holiness that may have rubbed off on us will have to be expressed in city terms. What you must do when the time comes for this correspondence to cease is to seek out and draw out a variety of lay Christians who have the whiff of genuine holiness and are immersed in the life of the world, from production-increasing top to football-kicking toe. Their lives, more than any words of mine, will make sense of 'holy worldliness'.

In the meantime I will take up your challenge, and try to write something for each of the forty days of Lent. It takes a pious mathematician or a figure-happy clergyman to know that the forty days from Ash Wednesday to Easter Saturday are forty days without the Sundays. I read it somewhere; but it can be checked. I shall suggest some Bible passages for the Sundays, and spread my letters over the days, each with a P.S. which you may interpret as postscript, passages of scripture, prayer and supplication, or 'pass the sanctity'.

Your discipline will be to read what I have written

and to do your homework as I have had to do mine. You may or may not keep the forty days in the process; that is for you to decide. I hope it will not seem too much like the dry wilderness, and I have said a prayer that you will sometimes strike the water-gushing rock.

Holy Joe

'I am holier than thou'

2

Thursday

Dear Joe,

How do we begin? Let us be honest, and confess to revulsion. Holiness! The word oozes hallowed stuffiness and haloed hypocrisy. Stand up the business man, bus man, or busy shopper, who will confess in the middle of High Street or at the middle of his own privacy to a desire to be holy. The word used in a city context has all the embarrassment of a resented intruder in the stock exchange or the suburban dance hall, the students' union or the trade union, the city club or the borough finance committee.

You, Joe, are exposing yourself by this strange interest to the sneers and snooks of people who regard themselves as healthy citizens with no nonsense about them. It was in the navy that the phrase 'holy Joe' originated. Is that what they called you? If they did, I am sure you bore the stigma stoutly. Jesus Himself suffered 'outside the gate', beyond the pleasantries and pats-on-the-back of civilized Jerusalem life. But never forget that some have been labelled 'holy Joes' not simply as a result of hostility to the cause of Christ, but through the insight of uncommitted but perceptive acquaintances who saw through the Pharisaic 'what-a-good-boy-am-I' plum-pulling and thumb-wagging. This is the kind of holiness which Isaiah identified and condemned as a holier-than-thouness. It is not only loathed by the man of the world, but detested by God. And for the Christian, quick-acting poison.

There are some who, sickened by superior sanctity of this kind, have gone away, ignorant that this brand of piety is not holiness but its demonic opposite. Others, prepared to make any contortions to avoid not only the appearance of evil but the appearance of holiness, have got twisted up in the attempt. Yet others have given close attention to our Lord's teaching that trumpets are banned, and have been so successful in muting their sacred music that only a few good ears have caught the authentic tone. How are we to know what is authentic holiness?

The difficulty is increased when we realize that whatever the words 'holy' and 'saints'—meaning 'holy persons'— imply, they are used in Scripture not for the specially devout, or spiritually gifted, or exceptionally mature, but for the 'ordinary Christian'; not for the blue-blooded holy Joe, but for every Tom, Dick, and Harry, Jane and Jennifer, who believes and is baptized. I remember an average young man in a Midlands city who, answering some questionnaire or other about something or other, was faced with the question, 'What is your main aim in life?' I wonder what my answer would have been. His was 'holiness'. To the plodding disciple it sounds too goody-goody. Yet this, or something with a strong dose of it, is the only Christian answer. We were called to this. This is that indispensable asset which alone makes it possible to 'see the Lord'. This is the single-minded life that goes with the many-dimensional Kingdom of God. This is what the Holy Spirit is after. This is the rarest and best of all discoveries, in ourselves or in others, in

to another age and a country environment.) Or, as those who think of a saint as one too pure to behold iniquity, strike out his eyes?

Kierkegaard's answer would be that we do nothing. Holiness is not in appearance at all. 'I draw closer to him, I watch every movement he makes to see whether he shows any sign of the least telegraphic communication with the infinite, a glance, a look, a gesture, an air of melancholy, a smile to betray the contrast between infinity and the finite. But no! I examine him from head to foot, hoping to discover a chink through which the infinite can peer through. But no! He is completely solid.'

Are we disappointed to learn that we may not recognize our city saint even if we find him? Or is there to be found here a clue, a most significant clue, to the chalk and cheese of 'holy worldliness'?

4

Saturday

P.S. You may welcome references to some of the things mentioned in my first two letters. I suspect that among the books you have been reading are Bonhoeffer's *Letters and Papers from Prison*, 1953, SCM Press, Daniel Jenkins' *Beyond Religion*, 1962, SCM Press, and John Robinson's *Honest to God*, 1963, SCM Press. If so, read them again, for they will take you a lot further than I can. Jenkin's book gives as an appendix the long passage from Kierkegaard about the 'knight of faith'.

The letter to Titus refers to worldliness and godliness —see 2^{11-14}. Paul tells his readers to copy him in many passages: 1 Thess 1^6, 2 Thess 3^5, 1 Cor 4^{16} and 11^1, Phil 3^{17} and 4^9. Try listing the things Paul considered worth copying, and ask how the modern urban Christian should copy them.

It is 'Hebrews' which says in 13¹³ that Jesus 'also suffered outside the gate'. The 'green hill', more likely to have been a rocky prominence, was 'outside the city wall'. The writer draws the conclusion, 'Let us then go to him outside the camp, bearing the stigma that he bore' (this to encourage suffering Christians) and nails home his argument by adding 'For here we have no permanent home, but we are seekers after the city which is to come.'

The Pharisaic attitude which takes even God's breath away is mentioned in Isa 65⁵. We compare Jesus' parable in Lk 18⁹⁻¹⁴. 'No trumpets' is recorded in Mt 6²⁻⁴. You remember telling me about the notice you once saw displayed outside the old law-courts in Lagos, Nigeria: 'No horns in Tinubu Square'. I think my comment was that this would make a good title for someone's autobiography, for in keeping the law we are unprofitable servants and horns are not appropriate. The notice reminds us that we are also forbidden to proclaim our presence outside the courts of Grace. Commentators have searched the historic records in vain for evidence that religious people did blow trumpets in the streets. Apparently Jesus did not expect to be taken literally; only seriously.

Heb 3¹ shows that holiness is for the ordinary Christian. The Greek has 'holy brothers' and the New English Bible translation presages my next letter to you. It reads 'Brothers in the family of God'. Heb 12¹⁴ insists that no man will see the Lord without holiness. What do you think is meant by 'seeing the Lord'? 1 Cor 3¹⁶⁻¹⁷ shows the Spirit dwelling in the 'holy temple'—us.

'The patience of a saint' was used in the House of Commons recently of our police force. It comes from Rev 13¹⁰, where it means something rather different,

and Job is singled out in Jas 5^{11}. Lk 1^{75} makes it clear
that holiness belongs to the whole of life; read also Rom
6$^{19\text{-}22}$ in the NEB. To discover what holiness is not, read
Mt 6$^{7\text{-}8}$ and 7$^{21\text{-}3}$. What else, according to Christ's
teaching, is holiness not? What, just at the moment, do
you think it is?

Self-examination

Lent—the season for repentance and fasting, an opportunity to use.

Repentance. What am I to repent of? Not just this little
pleasure that caused waste and proved empty; nor even
this large self-assertion that brought suffering. I repent
of a life that denies that God made me, contradicts that
the Spirit is working in me, and forgets that everything
is under the cross.

What has my calling as an ordained minister done to
me? How far has my life been a superficial copying of
the manner and motions that seemed appropriate? Have
I worked out my vocation in terms of entry into the world,
or escape from it?

What has your calling as a layman done to you? Have
you unconsciously assumed that because you are not a
minister or a missionary there are no equivalent sacrifices
that go with your calling?

Are we truly 'in the world', you and I? Our Lord
prayed that we might be, and that we might be kept from
evil. It is a great evil to contract out of life. Our Lord is
ascended in glory, and we would be with Him. Our
Lord is in the world, and we would be with Him.

What about fasting? Is there a destructive self-concern
to be put away for the rest of my life? Are there good
things which, in these forty days, must give way before

a sterner discipline? Should I take myself, and you yourself, more seriously—or less?

I am afraid of what will happen. I shall get sancti-monious, self-consciously pious. I shall be looking at myself instead of looking at God in others and others in God. I shall find it harder to do a spontaneous act of kindness, to raise an unpremeditated cheer, to enjoy things without introspection or an uneasy conscience.

I shall become a fussy do-gooder, even a turned-in feel-gooder. I shall miss the God-inspired ability to accept things as they are, to see them in their own terms and for their own sake. I shall be looking for hidden meanings, and miss the obvious beauty, the cause for laughter, the fresh insight, the job in front of me, the nascent relation-ship with another. I shall become dully devout, and a prize bore.

Who shall deliver me from this body of death?

Show us, O Lord, what it means to be holy.

Readings

I suggest the following Readings for the 1st Sunday in Lent (tomorrow). They link up with what I shall be writing to you about next week.

Ex 19[18-22]   The giving of community law
Heb 12[18-29]   The new community
Mt 5[43]–6[18]   The new law

Holy Terror

'Heard for his godly fear'

5

Monday

Dear Joe,

The target is holiness, and we have not yet come anywhere near it. What will help us to set out sights? Those who equate holiness with religious fuzz and ecclesiastical furnishings will be surprised to discover how easily the ways of the Kingdom can be illustrated by 'the children of this world'. Such a thing could not happen unless God had left His mark on us all. And it appears that the Holy Spirit makes regular nocturnal ventures into our affairs.

The moralist can produce his parables from nature because human life is so like animal life. Jesus could demonstrate the art of holy living by stories of city people who were 'no better than they ought to be' just because there are so many clues to the life of the Spirit in the 'natural' human order. Thus encouraged, I shall take my analogy from something you have written to me about from time to time, something about as far removed from conventional ideas on holiness as I can get—gang warfare.

You have seen evidence of gangs in the dock areas of city ports. Most towns have their share; mine certainly does.

Imagine a tough character who by virtue of the punch of his personality, and because he has made his base in the crypt of a deserted church, is called the 'Holy Terror'. He has gathered a gang around him, and has won—so far, and for the moment—their respect and loyalty. They admire his cool cunning, his cruel determination, and his casual power. Unaware of what is happening, they accept his 'code' and copy his mannerisms as the thing. They may grouse or kick, but they follow his dictates, privileged to get skewered on his whims and wants. The outsider —victim, parent, or magistrate—identifies them with their leader and calls them the Holy Terrors. Their business is to exploit the wealth and weakness of the world around them, to the advantage of their leader and themselves.

How does this sordid picture direct us towards holiness? Think first of the gang leader. He stands out. He dominates. He wears an aura of super-humanity. Unless and until he is shown up or thrown over, he bestrides their narrow world like a Colossus. He is godlike. Now when the psalmist keeps affirming that God is holy, and His Name is holy, he is saying that God has a life of his own, a uniqueness, a dreadful divinity, a terrible 'otherness'. The root idea of the Hebrew word which gives us 'holy', 'saint', 'sacred', 'sanctify', 'consecrate', is separation. So one scholar has said that holiness applies to 'that mystery in the Divine Being which distinguishes Him as God'; and another says that holiness is simply 'God-ness'. And as the 'Holy Terror' expresses his solitary leadership in big deeds, so God's Name is a strong Name, and His holiness is a supernatural power that acts and judges and delivers.

What we must not do is to let our analogy throw us to our childish nightmares of the God of the crushing hand, with the glint of stern judgment in His eye, and a mouth speaking words about us as hot as hell. The God Jesus reveals is one whose power is wholly directed to the ends of love. Jesus called Him 'Holy Father'.

Secondly, think of the Terror's cosh. No one would dare to touch it unless the Terror handed it to him. In Biblical thought anything that is 'near' to God shares the awful quality of His Being. This is similar to ideas of taboo which are common to many peoples. We could make a long list of things which are connected with the worship of Jehovah and which are called holy. Think of the ark, the temple vessels, the priests' clothes, and the sabbaths —all separated for the special use of God, all sharing His holiness.

I point this out because the most important of all the Terror's possessions is the gang itself. It shares his 'atmosphere'. It becomes an extension of his person and purpose. The members are tarred with his brush. With his power switched off, they look dusty; with it switched on, they dazzle.

God's people are God's 'holy people', by far the most significant of all His 'holy things'. The prophet says that when He raises up His 'sons' and establishes His covenant with them, He reveals Himself as 'the Holy One of Israel', and the heathen say of Israel 'Surely God is in thee.' When they have continually failed, a maiden called Mary is told 'that which is to be born shall be called holy'. And Jesus is presently recognized as 'the Holy One of God', and goes to His death 'heard for His godly fear' to raise up with Himself a new Israel, the Church, the 'holy people' of God inheriting all the promises. And you can see now that their call to be 'separate' is a call to belong to God, to be like God, to be enlivened by God.

6

Tuesday

To find the marks of a city saint, come a little further into the doings of the gang in the crypt. It will have its own rituals, its ways of talking and dressing and spitting, its methods of beating up and beating it, celebrations and punishments, all revolving round the boss. The book of Leviticus sets out the rituals which are to attend holiness. There is a correct way for the priest to perform every one of the acts of offering and sacrifice.

You will also find in Leviticus that ways of procedure in matters of the religious cult are put alongside duties in family, neighbourly and sexual relationships. These things, no less than the solemn rites, express holiness. Thus in one passage respect for parents immediately follows 'You shall be holy'. The parallel with the gang is here too. In addition to subtle ways of doing things, there is a gang spirit and a way of behaviour with its particular refinements and crudity, rough justice and corruption. Respect for parents is unlikely to be included; respect for 'old lags' may be. Some things are 'not done'. Some things are always approved. So with God's holy people and God's holy persons. There is a way of life and conduct which God approves, and to which all who are His are uncompromisingly committed: this is holiness.

The 'Holy Terror' will presumably approve the things that are 'in character' with himself, his views and his goings-on. It is the same with the Holy One of Israel. The holy life reflects the character of Him who is pure, just, compassionate, and faithful in all His dealings with the children of men. And the insistence that God's people should be holy, on pain of terrible retribution, is based on the rock-bottom affirmation of God's holiness: 'You shall be holy: for I the Lord your God am holy.' That is why the command in Leviticus is driven home like the harrowing hammering of nails into the coffin of human pride, independence, and self-satisfaction. 'God our Lord', says the prophet Isaiah, 'is sanctified in righteousness.' That would appear to mean that His glorious uniqueness is expressed in His relationship with His creation, and with you and me as part of that creation. We are to treat one another as He treats us.

All this finds a new height and depth, and a happy note of possibility, in the new covenant which is the subject of the New Testament. 1 Pet 1[13-22] quotes Leviticus and stresses the duty of obedience. But Peter looks to the final revealing of Jesus Christ. He was behind every revelation, but only now has holiness been fully seen in human flesh, only now is it possible in its fullest implications, and only now can the whole truth about every 'ordinary Christian' be told (verse 2). Hear the gang leader reminding one of his new boys of his privileges: 'Before you came in we hadn't got acquainted, you were clueless about real living and just a drifter. Now you've got me, and you know how to carry on, and you've something to live for. But you must be like me; I'll give you a hand.' That, or something like it, is how Peter hears the voice of Christ.

Note now two things about the dockland gang, both to do with its relationships with the world beyond. First, it finds opposition there from respectable citizens and other gangs. And second, it lives by what it can get from the outside world.

The Old Testament is full of tales of the enemies of Israel. They are derided by the writers of the psalms as also the enemies of God; nothing God does to them can be too severe. The Book of Revelation, written near the end of the 1st century, has a similar attitude to the persecutors of the Christian Church. Jesus was condemned as a gang leader and enemy of religious society. The charge brought against His followers in years of sharp martyrdom was that they were 'enemies of the human race'. There is a warfare of light and darkness. Men, said Jesus, must choose their leader. Yet God sends His rain on just and unjust, and God's holy people are to draw the full implications of His behaviour. All men are to be prayed for and ministered to, for God loves His enemies.

The other thing is more startling still. God's holy people were called into existence with the world in mind. Right back in the days when Abraham, going out into the unknown, was 'looking forward to the city with firm foundations', the promise was 'In thee shall all the families of the earth be blessed.' That golden thread is buried often, but never broken. Centuries later the book of Jonah speaks of the duties of the Jews towards the distant Gentiles. Both parts of 'Zechariah' end with the picture of all nations coming to worship at Jerusalem. Jesus, who confined His own ministry to the 'lost sheep of the house of Israel', looked to the day when they should come from all directions to sit down with Abraham in the Kingdom. The commission of God-contagious men has been to share God with all. They live for what they can give to the outside world. The people of the holy covenant are called together to make God their desire and the world their concern.

7

Wednesday

P.S. The reference to the 'children of this world' is in Lk 16[1-8]. You may like to think of examples from present-day city life of how people with no pretensions act more wisely according to their own lights than the 'saints'.

We see holiness expressed in powerful action in Isa 10[16-19]. How would you illustrate from the news this week? For one of many examples of a 'holy thing' used in ritual, note the 'holy crown' to be placed on Aaron's priestly mitre—Lev 8[9]. Lev 21[4-8] is a command for ritual holiness; Lev 19[1-3], a command for ethical holiness; while Isa 5[16] speaks of God's ethical holiness. Think of examples of the righteousness of God.

Two important passages about God's holy people are Deut 7[6-8] and 1 Pet 2[9]. The references to Christ Himself are Lk 1[35], Jn 6[69], Heb 5[7]. We read of the wider responsibilities of the 'holy nation' in Gen 12[3], and of God's attitude to the pagan city of Nineveh in Jon 4[10-11]. See also Zech 8[20-3] (about 520 B.C.) and Zech 14[18] (300-200 B.C.).

2 Tim 1[9-10] shows holiness as the gift of God. How am I to receive it?

The holiness of God Himself is fully recognized in Psalm 99 and Rev 4[8]. Vriezen says, 'The holiness of God is not only the central idea of the Old Testament, but also the continuous background to the message of love in the New Testament.' This is borne out by the passage on holiness in 1 Pet 1[13-17], where Peter adds to his injunction to holiness the warning that if we call God 'Our Father' we must stand in awe of Him (NEB).

'Hebrews' makes the same point, with a glorious contrast between the old and new ages—12^{18-29}. The untouchable, fearful mountain on which the Law was given has been replaced by the gracious and glorious city of God; but our God is still 'a devouring fire'.

Is this our attitude to the divine Love? If God—and how long a pause and how dedicated a life does one need, to get even a taste of the flavour of that word—if God has called me, mystery to myself as I am, to share His divine nature for His sake and the world's, this is awful! The physical toughness and brutality of the gang life we have been considering can give the feeling of 'Don't touch: 60,000 volts'. That is certainly how the Israelites felt about holiness. There was holy terror. And in the full light of the new dawn, we are still to worship God 'as He would be worshipped, with reverence and awe' (Heb 12^{29}).

Prayer

We can have no idea of what it is like to be God. We wonder if we have very much idea of what it is like to be man.

When we think of You as quite different from ourselves, then we are suddenly aware that You made man in Your likeness. When we speak as though You were a superman, then we are brought up sharply by all that has been said in our day about false and small images of Your true Being. Whether our thinking is done in the odd moments of reflexion, or in a life's work of systematic theology, we despair of our thinking about You. We are no longer sure what our words mean.

What we need is to experience You. But how? We are afraid of turning on our own emotions; we deplore self-deception. We are chary of religious experience, and wary of religious certainty. Yet we experience 'life'.

Are we so sure what that is? Every day and every night brings it. Is this, whether we know it or not, our experience of You?

You act in the mystery of Your Being. We act in the mystery of ours. What is God-ness at the adding machine or the printing machine or the washing machine? We can never be like You in Your power: to try to be is high blasphemy. Are we any more likely to resemble You in Your love: and are not our attempts at that also blasphemous?

Only You can impart the God nature, the family likeness, the gang solidarity. Holiness is You. Holiness is Yours to give, given with the Holy Spirit, given to Your people and to every member of the Body.

I stretch out my hands. I am conscious only of one thing—that they are trembling.

Holy Mountain

'the pattern shown you on the mountain'

8

Thursday

Dear Joe,

We are now faced with a question directed to this entire Lenten undertaking of ours. We have seen how the gang leader acts on his own initiative, gathers his boys around him, and puts the stamp of terror on them. God gives holiness whenever He draws something or someone into His life and influence. He gives it; it cannot be obtained any other way. Then what is the point in writing about holiness, if we can neither learn it, attain it, or approximate to it?

It would appear that God's gift of a holy life involves a call to work out in contempory and—for you and me—city terms, all that is implied by being joined to His 'gang'. We shall expect the Holy Spirit to speak to one man through another in this effort. Moses brought down from the holy mountain a pattern of living for his society, and the 'Ten Commandments' are still easier to learn than to keep. He also brought instructions about the place of worship, the tabernacle, down to the tiniest details of the candlesticks. We assume that God and he worked it out together. In our day the Holy Spirit gets His best results through the group, and few things are more vital for our Church fellowships than to wait upon

the holy God and discover the details of the outworking
of holiness.

Canon Douglas Rhymes has written that 'one of the
most important things of today is to try to find what
might be called a pattern of lay-holiness applicable to
the modern age'. He tells how he shared in a conference
of laity who 'wanted to work out for themselves, but
with the help of their clergy, what lay-holiness is, ... a
modern spirituality which is practical and realizable in
the world of today'. And then he adds a comment which
is worth chewing over: 'not monastic holiness or
theological college holiness or clerical holiness but lay-
holiness'.

Look at these special types first. Clerical holiness! You
will expect your minister or deaconess to show the signs.
What you must not do is to assume that this is the only
brand available, and that therefore either you are
exonerated, or you must imitate them to the best of your
poor lay powers and awkward lay circumstances.

If lay people would think deeper thoughts about clerical
holiness, less ordained men would be restless because of
patterns of life imposed upon them by lay neglect and
misunderstanding, patterns remote from theological
insights and current needs. You will see your minister
not, as someone has said, 'always isolated, whether in
holiness or hopelessness', but with his special share in
the holy Church which is set apart so as to be involved.
He is a gift of God to the Church. He will handle holy
things, and offer himself a holy sacrifice, 'to equip God's
people for work in His service'. He will be a means of
Christ's ministry to them, and will superintend their
ministry to the world. His example is the Good Shepherd
who both calls His own sheep by name, and leads them
out—for the pasture is out there on the hills, and city

saints are spiritually fed in noisy cafés, as well as at the silent family table.

You will not let your minister 'go out' alone; nor let him become so involved indoors that he cannot go himself, and knows too little of the world to guide his people out.

Because all are within holy Church, his pattern of holiness will not be in complete contrast to yours. He must pray for the flock; but so must you. And when he calls at your home your lives will touch, and the prayer will be common. Yet his 'use' is not yours. And you are to seek a lay holiness, distinctive, your own.

Nor will theological college holiness be your goal. I need hardly mention the differences in pattern; you are not in training for the ministry, nor relieved of the task of earning your living, nor living in college. But lay holiness will bear a strong resemblance to probationer-minister-holiness just because we all are under training.

It is not only theological students who must meet new ideas and disturbing thoughts. Our call to holy living in today's world includes an offering of mind and a mental discipline that is essential equipment.

'Training for a future ministry' is a phrase as applicable to the layman attending evening classes to 'better himself', as to a ministerial student. And ambition is consecrated as maximum availability to others.

College life is life in community kept warm by the sparks men rub from each other. Holy living will involve you, Joe, in intimate relationship with other Christians which public worship cannot provide, and the family and the 'fellowship' must.

The student's danger is losing touch with ordinary people, becoming a different person socially by the very fact of his education. Regular forays into the city, and reading novels of contemporary life and emotions, will help. The layman can live in a mental world more remote from life than any college. Make sure that your holiness is earthed.

9

Friday

What about monastic holiness? For many Protestants monasticism appears uncongenial and misguided. To them the monastery is a strange, remote world in which men or women contract out of their responsibilities and cut themselves off from the world. If that is true, there is monastic religiousness, but no monastic holiness.

More accurately, monastic life exists for the worship of God through the disciplined corporate life of those whose aim is sanctity for Christ's sake. Those so engaged know that worship is more than words and music, incense and bells, and keeping oneself unspotted from the world. They worship God through silence and work, by thought and compassion.

Even those communities which have the minimum of contact with life outside would relate their vocation to the 'full stream of the world' which they have apparently forsworn 'to live in a nook merely monastic'. One of the first and most famous desert hermits of the 4th century was visited by the equivalent of a reporter from the city he had left, and interviewed about his decision. What justification had he and his companions? He answered, 'We are guarding the walls'; that is, by our watchfulness in prayer we offer ourselves to Christ for the keeping of the city from evil. You, Joe, might prefer that they should have put up for the local elections; but do not miss the point that it was for the world's sake. Can everything that goes on in your local church be justified on the grounds that the city will benefit?

At the same time there is a monastic emphasis on personal salvation. Of course no follower of Christ can be ignorant that the way to save one's life is to lose it, and that this implies throwing life away for Christ in the least of His brethren. The Protestant layman and the Roman Catholic monk speak with one voice about sanctification; but they do not necessarily say the same thing. There is mutual misunderstanding here, happily being brought into the open in these days. When the Catholic denies that we are saved by faith alone, he is thinking of the necessity of sanctification, love, service, hope. But when the Protestant follows Luther in insisting on that word 'alone', the response of faith includes for him all those other things. There are still Methodists who have difficulty with the hymn-line, 'Through faithful service cometh full salvation'. But faithful service is (at any rate for those who live long enough) part of the response of faith.

We are taught to think of sanctification as a process, as though we could have more and more of it. But in the Bible it is a status, something that is true about us from the moment of 'justification' through the activity of Christ. This status is to be worked out in practical terms. The holy life is given; our business is to live it, rather to live it out—to exercise it in the sphere of our relationships and responsibilities. And the phrase beloved of John Wesley, 'entire sanctification', is the complete working it out.

Monastically this works out through the taking of vows. The pattern of lay holiness is not far removed from any one of them. You have not taken a vow of poverty, but you are the steward of your worldly possessions—and the present, inescapable duty of every Christian is to ask what is for him a Christian standard of living in a hungry world. You will interpret the vow of chastity as the full recognition that your body and mind are a temple of the Holy Spirit. You have made your marriage vows. It was a monk who showed me not only that celibacy is a Christian vocation with its own special value, but that marriage is equally a distinctive calling, in many ways a more complicated and challenging one. How many ministers live in the tension between work and home? It is a lay problem too, which may be resolved or intensified when we accept the married state unreservedly as our way of obedience. We need to remember this when we find ourselves objecting to a family life that prevents us praying with monastic regularity. How urgent it is at this point to find the pattern of lay, or married-minister, holiness.

The vow of obedience arises because every close-knit community needs authority, and the authority of Christ is delegated within His Church. The holy layman has no prior or council to bear the final responsibility, but he will work out his obedience with constant reference to holy things—Holy Scripture, Holy Church and its leaders to help interpret the mind of Christ, and the Holy Spirit bringing inner light. Many of us strongly feel the need of a 'rule of life', as Wesley did. It may be that a simple rule, as practised in the Renewal Group, will help laymen like yourself on the high road of holiness. You will not forget, as a Methodist with a Covenant Service, that you are committed to a life's service under solemn vows: nor that, for all the comparisons we have found, the holiness you seek is to be characteristically lay.

10

Saturday

P.S. Joe, I am afraid these postscripts are a bit demanding, but don't neglect them. 'Sources' are important, and I am glad of the chance of an extra comment.

The Ten Commandments are in Ex 20; the tabernacle and the candlesticks in Ex 25⁹ and Num 8⁴. The pattern is specially referred to in Heb 8⁵, where the writer says that our Christian worship is a copy of the heavenly pattern. I suppose he means that the principles of worship are eternally in the mind of God. Could this also be said of the pattern of lay holiness?

The quotation from Canon Douglas Rhymes is in his lecture on 'The Place of the Laity in the Parish' in a very stimulating book, *Laymen's Church*, 1963, Lutterworth Press. For the Church leader as God's gift see Eph 4¹¹⁻¹², from which the quotation comes. The RV is striking: 'for the perfecting of the saints (=holy ones) for work of ministering'. Ministers are not the only ministers. The Good Shepherd passage is Jn 10³, and note verse 16 'other sheep'. The 'nook' quotation is Shakespeare; I do not know which play. The hymn line is from William Vaughan Jenkins' hymn 'O loving Lord, who art for ever seeking'—M.H.B. 577.

My only personal glimpse of monastic life has been during a week spent with the Taizé community, in the heart of billowing, grape-growing Burgundy. Taizé is becoming more and more 'the thing' in forward-looking circles, but the life of the community goes quietly on. Taizé is that strange phenomenon, a Protestant monastic community. It consists of about sixty brothers, and there is a parallel community for women in Switzerland. Taizé began as the vision of a French-Swiss theological student, Roger Schultz, who set things moving in 1949 and is now the Prior. The brothers live in the village, side by side with villagers and farmers. They work with their hands and minds, and are self-supporting. There is a doctor, an architect, a farm-manager, potters and artists; and others who look after visitors, arrange retreats, and do the

chores. A few are ordained; most are laymen. Histori-
cally, monasticism has usually been a strong lay movement.

What impressed me so much about Taizé was the fact
of a strongly-bound community, determinedly open to
the world. The worship is available to all who come. And
a long line of parked cars and bicycle-strewn walls testify
the pull and power of it. I met up with a party of
twenty teenagers who had cycled from Switzerland and
were camping nearby to share three times a day in the
services.

This openness is also seen in the daily prayers for the
visible unity of all Christians 'that the world may believe';
in the remarkable links with the Roman Catholic authorities in an area where Protestants number two in a thous-
and; and in the growing contact with the Eastern
Orthodox Church which has chosen Taizé as its 'centre'
in the Western world and will shortly build a community
house there.

The world is much in view at Taizé. Some brothers
are away engaged in mission, in Ivory Coast, in Coventry.
The rest worship in a church at whose entrance a huge
sign proclaims in three languages, 'All you who enter
here be reconciled: Father to son, husband to wife, believer
to unbeliever, Christian to separated brother.' Here is a
community, not of withdrawal or escape, but of engagement. It describes its life as being 'at the crossroads of
the Church and the world'.

I left Taizé full of the scents of early summer and the
cadences of Alleluias. A very early Christian writer
described his vision of heaven as a garden of glorious
scents, and added 'So great was the perfume that it was
borne thence even unto us.' Taizé appeared to me like
that, its roots going deep, its influence wide. Can your
local Church have this openness to God and man? Can

its scent pervade the city smells with the fragrance of lay lives fulfilled in prayer and creativeness, reconciliation and labour, and the urban beauty of holiness?

From the Rule of Taizé

Perfect joy is in the laying aside of self in peaceful love; to burst forth, this joy needs all your being. Do not fear to share the trials of others, nor be afraid of suffering. For it is often at the bottom of the abyss that perfection of joy is given in communion with Jesus Christ. Perfect joy gives itself. . . .

Purity of heart can only be lived in spontaneous and joyous forgetfulness of self in order to lay down one's life for those whom one loves. This gift of oneself implies the acceptance of a sensibility often deeply wounded. There is no love of one's neighbour without the cross. The cross alone makes known the unsearchable depths of love. . . .

For the pure brightness of Christ to enter into you, it is not enough to gaze on it as though you were a disembodied spirit. You must commit yourself resolutely, in body and soul, on this way.

Readings

Readings for the 2nd Sunday in Lent could be as follows:

Amos 5$^{20-5}$ Justice in the city
1 Pet 2$^{1-21}$ The church a priestly community
Mt 5$^{13-16}$ The Church a visible city

Holy Priesthood

'a holy priesthood to offer spiritual sacrifices'

11

Monday

Dear Joe,

Characteristically lay! That is the holiness we are after. In the last letter we looked for our city saint in a monastery, and although we found traces of him, he still eluded us. What is the pattern of *lay* holiness? The colour and texture of that word 'lay' should help us. It is linked, as many writers and speakers are reminding us these days, with the Greek word 'laos' (two syllables) which means 'people' and is used regularly for 'the people of God'.

Ministers and children, monks and lay preachers, deaconesses and choristers, baptized mods and rockers, worshippers and elderly shut-ins, all belong to the 'laos'. And the 'laos' is called in Scripture a 'holy priesthood'. Lay holiness, apparently, is a priestly affair through and through. Unexpected? A paradox? We had better ask what is meant by a priest.

A priest is one who is in touch with God on behalf of others. He maintains the road between heaven and earth, and keeps the stream of two-way traffic going. It goes via him. Through him God comes to others, and they come to God. The very need of such a person drives home the Jewish conviction that God and man have fallen out, and their intended friendship broken down. In an industrial dispute the matter sometimes goes to arbitration. One side may suggest a way of settlement, and the arbitrator may follow this line of approach to success. If he does, something will be expected of both sides before relationships can be restored. That kind of thinking lies behind the Old Testament ideas of the work of a priest. God had provided a way—sacrifice. By this means, it was believed and hoped, three things could happen: God and man could again be at one (hence at-one-ment); man could offer to God himself (that was what he owed) through the best symbol of himself he could find—an animal without blemish; and God would give Himself (for that was man's need) through the supernatural life released. Always the priest offered the sacrifice as representative of others—often of all the people.

Through centuries of Israelite history we see this happening. God, through Moses, calls the whole nation to be 'a kingdom of priests'. This must mean a special task for Israel in relation to other nations—to be a go-between for God. In later years special groups are selected to perform the priestly tasks in Israel itself; they do it for the nation.

So we come to Christ Himself, a layman of Nazareth. His life shows Him up to be in a quite special sense the 'mediator', the 'way'. His words to the high priest at His trial about 'the right hand of power' hint at a new kind of priesthood, and later the Letter to the Hebrews develops this to show how He gathers up in Himself all that was meant by priesthood. The three things we noted are all there. He has made 'atonement'. He has offered a perfect offering, His own self obedient unto death. He has released the powers of the 'new age', the 'high life' of the Kingdom and the Spirit which He gives with Himself. He does this for others; is called 'the man for others'; represents in His priesthood the whole world, whose sin He has taken away.

So it is done. The religious ritual sacrifices are fulfilled, not by a ritual act, but by a life and a death and 'the power of an endless life'. 'He ever liveth to make intercession.' Then has the earth seen the last of priesthood? No, for the solitary figure on the cross, holding in one hand the life of God and in the other the life of man, is not the whole story. What we see is Him and His disciples. He called them to be with Him. He prayed for them when His hour of aloneness came. And afterward it was 'My Father and your Father'. It was 'It shall be told you what you must do.' The one and only Priest has a Body on earth, a community to live out His priestly ministry to the world. To the world!

Such is the 'laos', the holy people called 'a royal house to serve as priests'. As with the royal house of centuries before, it is the world they represent before God. The controversy stirred up by the Anglican-Methodist proposals on this subject of priesthood must not blind us to the summary of fundamentals in the Report. The statement, having said that through Christ alone God reconciles the world to Himself, continues,

'By sharing in his priestly ministry, the Church corporately is a royal priesthood, a holy nation. In and under Christ it offers God's pardon and grace to the world, intercedes with God for the world, and offers itself and its worship as a living sacrifice to God.'

To the world! For the world! Holiness and the world could not be brought into closer proximity. And one way or another, we are to see them together in the life of a city saint.

12

Tuesday

The Church 'offers itself and its worship'. Our next
letter must be concerned with worship. In what remains
of this one we must ask how the priestly community is to
offer itself on behalf of the world, and where the city
saint comes in.

We thought of the work of the priest making the sacrifice
in three ways. First it dealt with guilt and separation.
There are times, no doubt, when the city knows that it is a
'bloody city', as Fox called Lichfield; and it looks round
warily, waiting to be told so. Its guilt, in the first place,
is not in its quarter-full churches, but in its heart-less
hearts and its life-less lives; not so much in beer and bingo
as the refusal to admit corporate responsibility. When, in
Fry's *Thor with Angels*, Cymen the Jute chief asks forgiveness for the sorrow of the world, his daughter says,
'You haven't made the sorrow'. He replies,

> 'All make all:
> For while I leave one musle of my strength
> Undisturbed, or hug one coin of ease
> Or private peace while the huge debt of pain
> Mounts over all the earth,
> Or, fearing for myself, take half a stride
> Where I could leap; while any hour remains
> Indifferent, I have no right or reason
> To raise a cry against this blundering cruelty
> Of man.'

The Church has its own forms of 'private peace' and
indifference and blundering kindness needing atonement;
but its activities in the world, and the life of every city
saint, must show what forgiveness means in terms of man
and God.

Secondly, the priest offers the sacrifice on behalf of those who bring it. It is the world's life that is to be brought. And when Churches organize Christian Aid Weeks, and when priestly members get deeply immersed in Community Associations and specialized service and neighbourly acts, they are out to make the offering a worthier one.

The gift was sanctified, made holy, when it was placed on the altar. So every city situation, every element of work and relaxation, every political and personal responsibility, every conversation and act of will, cries out to be made holy. For holiness belongs to God, and all these things are to be brought into relationship with God, His obligation of love, and His promises of peace. That is their deliverance and fulfilment, and Christ insists upon involving His people in this process, for they have been separated from the world in order to hallow the world.

As for the 'life in the blood', new-springing life is to flood the world through the sacrifice of Christ-in-His-people. Many people inside and outside the Church think of it as a sobering influence, forgetting that in the 'new age' water becomes wine and that new wine-skins (that is, fresh institutions and patterns of life) are continually needed to contain it.

Roger Tennant draws the lesson from Paul that we must take our choice—to be drunk with wine or with the Spirit; no third possibility is worth considering! Somehow or another we must show that we are alive—whether by natural exuberance or spiritual effervescence.

In villages of another generation, and in some modern suburbs lacking social facilities, we see the church as a centre of bubbling activity. In a thousand other directions today Christians are needed to provide, not the brake, but the acceleration and the steering. In secular youth clubs and community centres and wherever you look in the city, men and women are needed who live well and purposefully.

The trouble with city Christians is not only that they so well merit the adjectives 'respectable' and 'middle class'—which can only be transcended by contact with the mature revolutionary Jesus Christ; the trouble is that the picture of 'God-ness' they present is so dull. Who with life in his veins would choose a life so church-tied, care-ridden, and conscience-stricken? The city saint must, he must, have the full attractiveness of one who enjoys life immensely. So Kierkegaard says of his 'knight', 'His appetite is stronger than Esau's', and again, 'He takes pleasure in all things, takes part in everything, and everything he does, he does with the perseverance of earthly men whose souls hang fast to what they are doing.'

In all these things, the 'holy priesthood' will be as intimately related to the world's life as the Levitical priest was to those for whom he offered sacrifice; and yet still be one with the High Priest, from whom all priesthood derives, who gave Himself to be a Victim not only as sacrifice but also as example.

13

Wednesday

P.S. The other day I had the excitement of opening a bottle taken from the foundations of a church building demolished in the city re-development. In it was a daily paper of 14 July, 1873 giving the programme of a Church congress soon to be held at Bath. The subject of the first session was 'The Church's duty in regard to strikes and labour'. But it was the topic for the first evening meeting

lively life of Christ called *Born of a Woman*, 1961, SPCK. For the blood as the seat of life, see Gen 9[4] and marginal references. There is a phrase of Glover in his book *The Jesus of History*, so often quoted in my student days that I hesitate to give it. But a new generation has arisen— yours. The phrase can hardly be bettered when we are thinking about the abundant life. Glover says that the early saints 'out-lived, out-thought and out-died' their contemporaries.

Finally, think quietly on these words of Aristides about the laity of A.D. 140: 'Because they acknowledge the good-nesses of God towards them, lo! on account of them there flows forth the beauty that is in the world. And truly they are of the number that have found the truth. And to me there is no doubt but that the earth abides through the supplication of the Christians.' Presumptuous? Perhaps. But . . .

Holy Sacrifices

'intercessions and thanksgivings offered for all men'

14

Thursday

Dear Joe,

All those who are currently 'with it' theologically juggle with Bonhoeffer's phrase 'religionless Christianity': another unexpected marriage of words. It seems that the Holy Spirit has a particularly strong word to say to us on this subject. My last letter may have pointed you that way. If the ritual acts of the Old Testament priest have been fulfilled in the earthly and heavenly activity of Christ, then the day of sacrifices is over. 'Religion', which we may define as all those special cultic activities which are meant to link God and man, would appear to be a misuse of energy. Jesus Himself, following a recurring prophetic theme, said that God desired mercy, not sacrifice. And in any event, says 'Hebrews', the perfect sacrifice of life in death has been made for good. So, the argument runs, let us get on with living, for it is in life that we meet and serve God. Such an exhortation comes as a relief to those who are depressed by the unreality that goes with much public worship and many devotional meetings.

Yet the truth is that while the New Testament uses religious language of the worship of life ('offer yourselves a living sacrifice') it also stresses the 'sacrifice of praise'. And the 'holy priesthood' is given the words and actions of Holy Communion in the church, as well as of holy communion in the city.

Human beings are talking-and-thinking animals. We use words to convey something to others, and words bring new knowledge and experience to us. The lover says 'I love you' and the worshipper hears 'Holy, holy, holy'. God speaks to us in events, and we reply by actions. But His acts and ours have a meaning, and we can think of His Word ('Logos' in Jn 1[1]) as either an active-word or a deed-with-meaning. Words are important in any covenant, including a holy one—important especially to those who are called not servants, but friends.

The words, I think, should—except for traditional prayers—be in the language of our day and place; and we shall not forget that there are other ways than words for God's impression and our expression. It was a small girl at bedtime who said she wanted to dance her prayers; it has been done in Coventry Cathedral.

We should not be surprised, then, to find that Kierkegaard says of his 'knight of faith', 'On Sunday he takes a holiday. He goes to church.' Behind that simplest of statements lies all the ecclesiastical machinery of institutional church life; also the mysterious purpose of God in creating a universe, producing a human race, and gathering a worshipping community.

Why does he go to church? To acknowledge the holy God on behalf of himself and others who do no such thing; and to offer himself with his fellow-Christians for those others. To put it another way: In worship the Church speaks as the priestly representative of the world before God; and at the same time accepts God's call to priestly activity in the world. Look at the first of these with me.

The Church is called into existence for the sake of an

estranged world. It is to be articulate on behalf of a stuttering race; to shout aloud in the name of a silent planet; to worship the true God representing an idolatrous generation.

On his way to church, the city saint passes cars with L-plates front and back, driven by men not learners of Christ. On the pavement waiting for buses are fishermen equipped for weather and waiting, who have not heard the call to be fishers of men 'come wind, come weather'. What goes on in church while they change gear or bait, is for them.

Karl Barth writes, 'While we are in communion with the saints, the ecclesia of those who are gathered together by Jesus Christ, we are also in communion with those who, perhaps, do not pray as yet but for whom Christ prays, since He prays for all mankind. When Christians pray they are, so to speak, substitutes for all those who do not pray; and, in this sense, they are in communion with them, in the same way as Jesus Christ has made himself one with sinful man and lost humanity.'

There may sometimes be little in worship to remind the Christian of this: that may be one reason why it may seem a burden to be endured rather than the chance to bear another's burden. A recent statement on worship describes it as 'an affair between the world and God, via us'. When we realize how easily worship can be a beautifully paved cul-de-sac, or even a road closed at both ends, the privilege of that 'via' is immense.

15

Friday

The second motive for worship is the corporate offering of the life of the 'saints'. Harvest Festivals and Industrial Sundays remind us that what we offer primarily is our life in the secular world. As the sabbath for the Jew, so every Sunday is meant to be not just a holy day different from the others, when the Christian 'takes a holiday', but a day representative of 'seven whole days'.

I once heard a farmer speak of life in the country, and of the sense he had of contributing to the world's interdependent life. He said that the finest experience this side of life (as he put it) was standing on a back of a tractor, supervising the seed-drill, and revelling in a dry autumn day. Good luck to him. Industrial society provides the tractor, but the thousand trades of the city can obscure the fact of 'contributing'.

That seed-drill, it appears, was invented by a city lawyer driven to country exile by ill-health. He took up agriculture and organ playing. In church one Sunday his eyes lingered on the organ pipes. He suddenly saw them doing another job—sowing seeds—and the sound-box of the organ became the seed-box. The seed-drill had arrived.

Should he have been concentrating more on the business in hand? There is a sense in which it is impossible to have wandering thoughts in prayer, for every thought has significance and can be interpreted 'on the God-ward side'. Perhaps the class meeting suffered because in the sharing of experience 'religious' thoughts seemed appropriate, and one seldom heard, 'I have just had a good idea about what to buy my husband for Christmas', or 'Now I know what to say to my employee whose home is breaking up'. I am not suggesting that worship is a means to making business more efficient or home life more liveable; but rather that when we meet the living God He talks to us about field and factory, home and school, His holy Word being grounded in our daily circumstances and needs. Our response is about those things too.

The Church offers something else: its life in priestly

ministry for the world. The best place in the service for
this to be made crystal clear is the Notices. Enough said.
I sometimes wish that for an hour before the act of worship, the congregation could engage in what would be
a 'Conversation on the work of God', with God's holy
will and our local responsibility as the theme. 'Who
will visit young Tom in hospital this week, and who will
place chess with old Dick (we know why he gets so cross
when he loses), and who will transport Harry's wife
to the clinic? Who will represent us at the parent-
teachers meeting, and who at the local group studying
housing? No, Mrs Jones, we realize that you cannot go
anywhere without being taken; but we shall pray tonight
for six people in great need, and this will give you your
daily half-dozen. Are there any others who should be
prayed for throughout the week?' And just as worship
during some special campaign has a relevance and freshness, so with such a 'preliminary' the point of what we are
doing would be unmistakeable.

The Sacraments set the pattern here. The city saint
became a priest at his baptism. A layman leading
intercession in my church prayed that God would make
all the young people of the congregation into good
trustees! Something is spiritually wrong when people are
not ready to accept such jobs; but the new life tokened
in baptism finds expression in a diversity of gifts. The
'faithful soldier and servant' fights on a wide front, and
serves in the city and the world. In the Book of Common
Prayer the godparents are told that they must teach the
child the significance of what has happened, and to this
end 'ye shall call on him to hear sermons'. The aim is 'a
Christian life . . . daily proceeding in all virtue and godliness'. This child is a new gift of God to the world, and
the Church of South India prays 'that he may go forth'.

When people speak of the liturgical movement, they refer to the new-old understanding of the congregation in Holy Communion making itself available to God for His tasks. We must admit that Cranmer's service is not as helpful as it might be in stressing that the Father is seeking worshippers and that the Church accepts anew its commission at the family table. Yet the collect of preparation draws no boundary smaller than the entire race ('unto whom all hearts be open'), and the Gloria insists that our Centre is the Lamb of God who takes away the sin of the world. The prayer of intercession takes up the instruction to Timothy to pray and give thanks for all men. We pray with all men in mind because Christ has them in mind. Modern liturgies are making this clearer.

The shared commission of the Church is expressed in strongly corporate worship. Kierkegaard says of his 'knight', 'his healthy bellowing of the psalms proves only that he has got a sound pair of lungs'. But it could also prove that he is enthusiastic in taking his part both in the coming-in and the going-out. Certainly he will find a life's obedience in the simple dismissal from the Communion Table 'Go in peace'. Go—not just back to your seat, or home to your family and the television, but 'out there' where the worship of word and the worship of life are one holy sacrifice of soul and body.

16

Saturday

P.S. The emphasis on life rather than religion is in Hos 6[6], quoted by Christ in Mt 12[7]. Professor C. R. North comments on Heb 10[19-24], 'The only Jew who could ever enter into the Holy of Holies on earth was the High Priest. Laymen were never allowed even into the earthly sanctuary. But Christ opened up and dedicated

a way, a new and living way, for all the children of men,
including—we must assume—laymen, women, and Gentiles, who come to him with a true heart and in fullness of
faith, into the very sanctuary of God in the heavens.'
This 'way' is a way of faith and life, not of ritual. The
preceding passage, Heb 10[11-18], says that 'there is no more
offering for sin'. But verse 25 insists that we must still
meet. Liturgical language used of life is found in Rom
12[2] and 15[27], Acts 13[2], Phil 2, 17 and 30.

The quotation from Barth is in *Prayer and Preaching*, SCM
Press, p. 25. The 'via' statement is from World Student
Christian Federation literature. The phrase 'on the God-
ward side' was used by Nairne in 'The Epistle of Priesthood' to translate the Greek word in Heb 2[17] which RV
gives as 'in things pertaining to God'. Everything that
we see and touch has a God-ward side. Bishop Stephen
Neill has written that the Church stands on the God-ward
side of the universe.

Can worship be a 'means' to a good end? The worship
of God is the 'end' of human existence, but worship-in-
church can certainly be a 'means'. To what end, Joe?
It is interesting that John Wesley dared to call the love
of God 'the most powerful Means of Health and Long
Life'.

'A priest at his baptism.' 1 Peter, which stresses priesthood in chapter 2, is regarded by many scholars as based
on an address on baptism. The link between baptism
and witness is strongly presented in believers' baptism.
In the Church of South India service the charge is given,
'Let us therefore bear witness to the world that Christ is
our life'. For Churches that practise infant baptism,
Confirmation is the initiation of the 'full member' (though
not all traditions think of it so). The Methodist practice

has been to offer 'the right hand of fellowship' which stresses the welcoming *in*, but the laying on of hands goes deeper, especially if Acts 13[1-3] is in mind.

The corporate mission of the Church is made quite explicit in modern liturgies. One ends by applying the words of Christ, about His vocation, to His sent Church: 'The Spirit of the Lord is upon me, for He hath anointed me to . . .' Those of us who are still becoming familiar with Cranmer's order should welcome at the end of the service a hymn of mission such as M.H.B. 590.

If worship is the consciously offered life of Church in community, should Christians within a group, whether it be a factory or a voluntary society, pray together?

The question was raised concretely for me the other day when a keen young Christian girl who has led a rather sheltered church life complained to me that worship had lost its freshness. I suggested that she was spending too much time on church premises, and that she ought to be getting out more. She later came back to say that she had been to the Young Conservatives, but was very disappointed because there had been no 'Epilogue' in the meeting!

I can see why Christians in college or office want to pray together in the lunch-break, but I think it can be very easily overdone, and may hinder the Christian mission. It is interesting that the Campaign for Nuclear Disarmament has its Christian group which meets for prayer; but the prayer has in mind not so much fellow disarmers as a world 'on the brink'. House-fellowships run by Churches, if they are really getting in neighbourly non-church-goers, should be very reluctant to include prayer on the informal agenda. The one group about which one would give an unqualified Yes to corporate

prayer is the Christian family; but only if all the members
are Christian.

Use today a prayer used by the Renewal Group:

Almighty God, our heavenly Father, who dost set
forth Jesus Christ to be the High Priest, Shepherd and
Head of thy Church; grant that, looking unto him, we
and all thy people may enter into the perfect worship of
his eternal sacrifice, the ministry of his yearning love, and
the unity of his blessed body; that thy Church may be
holy as he is holy, and glorify thee, Father, Son and
Holy Spirit.

Readings

Suggested Readings for the 3rd Sunday in Lent:
1 Sam 9   City of Ramah
Rev 3[7-13]   Message to city of Philadelphia
2 Tim 3[12-17]; 1 Tim 6[3-11]   The man of God
Mt 11[16-19]   City marketplace

Holy Prophets

'there is in this city a man of God'

17

Monday

Dear Joe,

When we were thinking of the kind of conversation that might well go on before worship, you may have noticed that we were talking about the prophetic as well as the priestly work of the Church. The prophet's business is to proclaim God's Word, and in the Old Testament this overlaps with the priest's task of being the 'way' between God and man. Samuel combined both.

Which reminds me. I once attended Evensong in the cathedral of an industrial city. The reader of the First Lesson was a clergyman notorious for his political activity. He read from 1 Sam 9 the long story of Saul the son of Kish looking for his father's asses: the set passage for the day. In the presence of numbers of visitors, few of whom were probably regular church-goers, I grew more and more restless. I knew as you would have done that we were hearing about an incident of high moment in Israelite history. This was the beginning of kingship, of a road leading to David and beyond him to one of David's line. But this was not clear from the Lesson, and no explanation was given. At that moment I burned for clearer indications that the Word is spoken to city men now, as to wayfarers then.

Samuel, as priest and prophet, exerted not only a city
but a national influence. If we ask where the prophetic
witness is today, a number of answers could be given. We
can think of a few outstanding Christians in public life
of whom it may be said, as of Samuel, 'he is a man that
is held in honour'. There are less than formerly in my
city. Is the cause lethargy, or the suspicion that politics
is 'a dirty game'? St Augustine noted long ago that
because of inevitable compromises involved in government, 'the holy men of old were shepherds of cattle
rather than kings of men'. Had he forgotten Samuel?
To those who take the political plunge, the Church has a
delicate and urgent responsibility. A man or woman
who is not regularly in the pew and at the 'fellowship'
may quickly get neglected, even written off.

But of course the modern equivalent of Samuel is the whole
Church, sharing the prophetic calling of its Lord. Moses'
prayer was 'Would God that all the Lord's people were
prophets, that the Lord would put his spirit upon them',
and it was answered on the day of Pentecost. But what
comparison is possible between Samuel in Ramah and
the Church in the city? We must not skate over the
judgment of Lewis Mumford, who knows about cities:

'In the metropolis today the Church is a survival:
its power rests upon numbers, wealth, *material* organization, not upon its capacity to give its stamp to the daily
activities of men: it claims much, but except by repetition
and rote, it contributes little to the active spiritual life
of the city.'

This loss of influence goes with the development of
secular society over centuries. Drama is one illustration
of many an activity that broke loose from the Church's
apron strings and revelled in its new independence; or
there could not have been Shakespeare. And drama today

is a powerful example of how God is active outside the
bounds of His holy prophets to speak a word about who
and where we are—a contemporary 'Samuel' announcing
both man's kingship and his lostness, for the fourth part
of a shekel of silver.

Compared with the cities we live in, Ramah was a rural
community. The Church has far to go before its prophetic
witness is geared to the city. A curate here tells me that
as many people live in one street in his parish as there
were living in his previous country parish. But boundaries
and staffing are at least coming under scrutiny. And the
'rural dean' is the bishop's industrial chaplain. Yet
still the content of many of our Sunday services would
fit almost any time and place, instead of being grounded
in God and in the modern city.

We must not too readily accept the comment that the
Bible is difficult because it belongs to country life. Not
all of it is about hill country and lost asses. Indeed, the
city of Jerusalem comes to dominate Old Testament
prophecy, and the fourth Gospel shows us how much of
Jesus' ministry was in the city. The Gospels are associated
with cities, and most of the New Testament letters are
addressed to city Churches. And, of course, 'it ends with
a city of gold'.

The letter to Philadelphia in Rev 3[7-13] shows a
prophetic view of the city. The 'open door' reference
arises because Philadelphia had been built as a gateway
to the East for the spread of Greek culture. Every city
is a gateway to other realms, from which goods and
men, cultural ideas and social habits, are exported. And
to the city saints God still shows the opportunities He
gives His Church. The Holy One says, 'I have set before
you an open door, which no one can shut.' Doors must
be passed through.

18

Tuesday

To accept fully his opportunities, the city saint must meet the requirements for a prophet: the knowledge of God's Word and of the world he lives in. And because God is at work in contemporary events, he will find that God's Word is *in* them, not just about them. Samuel was gifted not only with supernatural knowledge, but with the knowledge of asses and kings.

What is the city really like? One side of its life is portrayed by Raymond Chandler in *The Little Sister*. The investigator Philip Marlowe says that Los Angeles was once 'good hearted and peaceful', but now the 'hoodlums' have come:

'We've got the flash restaurants and night clubs they run, and the hotels and apartment houses they own, and the grifters and con men and female bandits that live in them . . . the riff-raff of a big hard-boiled city with no more personality than a paper cup. Out in the fancy suburbs dear old Dad is reading the sports page in front of a picture window, with his shoes off, thinking he is high class because he has a three-car garage. Mom is in front of her princess dresser trying to paint the suitcases out from under her eyes. And Junior is clamped on to the telephone calling up a succession of high school girls that talk pidgin English and carry contraceptives in their make-up kit.'

His companion comments, 'It is the same in all big cities, amigo.' He answers, 'Real cities have something else, some individual bony structure under the muck.'

In such a city, saints will need to be tough, and Churches available to provide the backbone under the muck. And the Word of God is there to be discovered,

unless all the prophets are too busy getting lost within
the prophetic community. The modern city is producing
a new kind of man, and new types of society, and the
prophet must have a deeper understanding of the world he
shares in than others do. He will need to be living the
life, not remote from it. He will know something of the
confidence and the bewilderment, the casualness and
earnestness, the strength and inner turmoil, of his fellow-
men. He will join with others to study the flesh and
bone of industry. He will find the time to go regularly to
extra-mural classes or their equivalent, dealing with
many facets of his life and that of his contemporaries.
He will not make piety a cloak for ignorance. He will
thank God for William Temple College and the Luton
Industrial Mission, and use them first to discover himself.
And if he does not know what it is like to live in tall flats
like long vertical streets of houses where no one passes,
he will try to find out.

In such a world, says 2 Tim 3, the man of God will draw
truth from the sacred writings 'which have power to make
you wise'. And by this means he will be 'efficient and
equipped for good work of every kind'.

God's Word is found in Scripture, for here is the record
of how God has acted and spoken in events, from the
beginning of creation until now. The Word, centred
on Jesus Christ, is already given; and all life and thought
is to be guided and tested by this unsurpassable revelation.
And the commuter who goes by electric train, as well as
he who runs, may read.

But let him read in three necessary ways. First, when
he reads the Bible he must not stop being an urban scien-
tifically-minded man living in a secular society. The two
worlds mentality is enervating for a person, and dis-
astrous for a prophet. Let him look constantly for the

light he needs, but not object that the light comes through the prism of his conditioned mind. That is how it has always come to the prophets. The light is for his condition. God speaks to this age.

Secondly, let him take every advantage of modern scholarship. You must not say to him, 'Read the Bible, not books about the Bible'. For he needs the Bible in a form he can take, and the best books about the Bible will send him to the Bible with freshened interest and a comprehensive view. Countering the unavoidable idiosyncrasies of scholars, he will unashamedly rack their brains, and will grow as interested in 'Q' and oral tradition as he is in his wife's childhood. He will not despise the use of an electronic brain to help determine facts about the authorship of biblical books—though he will insist that the brain power is adequate. He will be fascinated to find out how and what his children are taught in school R.I. lessons and Sunday School classes.

Lastly, he will read knowing that the response required is more than understanding. He may read about holiness, but unless he follows an insight, obeys a directive, and acts on a revelation, he will have glimpsed a route-map, not travelled its ways. He will also recognize that many of his contemporaries are biblically illiterate, and—like Mohammed of old—have only the Christians to interpret to them through life what God is saying. Mohammed had no Bible in his language, and only knew a shoddy Church—so he looked for other light. A similar thing is happening today. Can it also happen that the modern equivalent of the man of God, which is Christ-in-His-Church, will be heard by city men to say 'Stand thou still at this time, that I may cause thee to hear the word of God'.

19
Wednesday

P.S. The decline of the Church's influence in our country is examined by F. C. Mather in *The Layman in Christian History*, 1963, SCM Press, a supermarket of information. See pages 232, 233 for the aloofness of Churches and Chapels to social and political issues. He adds that this 'has itself prompted new lay initiatives, many of them ecumenical in character, reflecting and assisting the growing unity among the Churches . . . For it has come to be realized with increased conviction that only through a fully active laity can the Christian faith make any real impression upon the contemporary world.'

It is not only the Church which has not caught up with our urban civilization. My son has just received Dorothy Clewes' *Skyraker and the Iron Imp*, the adventures of a crane; cranes being as thick in this city as trees in the forest. Yet the *Times Educational Supplement* review pointed out how few children's books speak the language of city life. Animals and country scenes still predominate.

This is certainly true of our hymns. A whiff of exhaust fumes (refreshing for once) comes with 'Now let us remember the joys of the town', but there will have to be better city hymns than this. What we need is a spate of gallant attempts out of which one or two would gain recognition and immortality. There is some indication that this is happening, and only this week a religious journal published the latest one, by Richard G. Jones, beginning

'God of concrete, God of steel
   God of piston and of wheel
God of pylon, God of steam
   God of girder and of beam
God of atom, God of mine
   All the world of power is thine!'

Incidentally the cities with which the Gospels are linked are these: Rome with Mark, Antioch with Matthew, Alexandria with Luke, and Ephesus with John.

There are many examples of how the writer of the seven letters in Revelation 1–3 recognizes that his readers live in an urban society. To Smyrna, a city ringing the lower slopes of a hill and hence called 'the crown of Asia', he speaks of the crown of life (2^{10}). The terms of Laodicea, with its banking, its cloth factory, and its eye hospital, are bitingly relevant (3^{17-18}). The best picture of all is the letter to Philadelphia, which I quoted in the letter, which Dr Barclay calls 'a unique example of how to use the here and now to get to the there and then'. (Not that prophecy is only about the 'there and then'. It is also about the God-ward side of the 'here and now'.) Read it through—Rev 3^{7-13}. And then join with me in a thanksgiving based on verse 12 (NEB).

Thanksgiving

The Christian here, as throughout these three chapters, is described as 'he who is victorious'. Earthly cities are part of the world which Christ the Victor has overcome. We are now 'more than conquerors in His love' and complete victory is assured.

And so the prophet mentions four things about our destiny— all of them also saying something about what we are now.

'Pillars'. Philadelphia honoured its public benefactors by inscribing their names on the pillars of the (pagan) temples. We still use the phrase—'pillars of the Church'; and it means 'honoured members' not 'supports'. The humblest saint will have an honoured place in the presence of God; he has it now.
I pause, and give thanks.

'He shall never leave it' is a reference to the unsettled life of people living in an earthquake-prone area. Time and again refugees had to 'go out'. Cities were built to provide security; cities today are vulnerable, and salvation is only in God. Beatniks have left modern civilization in disgust; they have their reasons. The presence of God is secure and entirely satisfying. Is and will be.

I pause, and give thanks.

'The name of my God', 'my own new name'. Philadelphia had at one time been renamed 'Neocaesarea' in honour of Tiberias who gave much help to the rebuilding of the city after a particularly devastating earthquake. A new name to mark an imperial generosity. Name implies nature, and our Christian name proclaims God's gracious activity in giving the new life of the Spirit, now and presently in fullness.

I pause, and give thanks.

'The city of my God'. God's perfect will is a community. All communities are already His. One day He will give that city of which every city is the foretaste and sign. Including mine.

I pause, and give thanks.

> 'Lord, look upon us in this city,
> And keep our sympathy and pity
> Fresh, and our faces heavenward—
> Lest we grow hard.'

Holy Nation

'come away and leave them, separate yourselves'

20

Thursday

Dear Joe,

The prophet must not only know his world, but live as part of it; and the city saint will not only try to understand the community but rub shoulders with others in it. This means being involved, even immersed. We find a strong reluctance within the Church in many parts of the world to accept this. Students in newly independent countries are apparently no exception. The entire colourful cloth of their life is woven with politics, yet very many keep aloof, giving Christian discipleship as their reason. We noticed in my last letter a similar thing happening in our country. Why is this?

The conception of holiness has something to do with it. The word means 'separate', and when the Israelites are told to come out and be separate there is a geographical reference in it. For the Christian the separation is from everything 'worldly'. We may be able to examine that word more closely later. Its current use is almost always in a bad sense, following the scriptural belief that the world God made has fallen into bad ways, and is out of step with God's will. Everything that shares in this rebellion against divine government is called 'worldly', 'of the world' and needs to be rescued. The baptized person is committed to renounce 'the world' in its estrangement from God, and 'worldliness' is used for everything he has turned his back on.

So the fear of compromise may keep a Christian at arms length from life. He will pay his taxes, though he may not agree with all government expenditure. He will be involved in joint action, in industry or society, with which he will not fully agree. He may not realize how much compromise is necessary to remain in the world of organized society at all. But he may try to keep 'doubtful' contacts to the minimum.

A second reason for keeping separate is the danger of bad influence. This seems to be very much behind the stringent rules that developed in Judaism: those pagans were always leading God's people up blind and blasphemous alleys. So we have to advise children and tender Christians to choose their friends carefully. A hard-grained bad-un at a boys' home (he was sixteen) told me that he had been sent there in the hope that some of the other boys would improve him. 'It works the other way,' he grinned, 'I make them worse.' Jesus knows what is in man, so He prays that His disciples may be kept from evil —but not that they may be taken out of the world. Then there is the matter of reputation. We do not want ourselves or our cause to get a bad name. Birds of a feather, you know. St Paul puts forward strong views against the marriage of Christian and pagan, and we see the point of that especially in the kind of society for which he wrote. But apparently he was misunderstood. In 1 Corinthians he mentions a previous letter in which he said that his readers must have nothing to do with 'loose livers'. Now he is at pains to insist that when he wrote that he was not thinking of *pagans* who are 'grabbers and swindlers or idolaters'. He drily comments, 'To avoid them you would have to get right out of the world'.

It is loose-living Christians who are to be avoided—
people who give the Church a bad reputation.

We should not be surprised at Paul's attitude. He
has the example of Jesus. The warning of Proverbs to
the good Jew could not be clearer:

> 'Be not among winebibbers;
> Among gluttonous eaters of flesh.'

Yet the way Jesus behaved is also quite clear. That,
says St Matthew, is exactly what He was. His reputation
could not be worse: He was actually the friend of tax-
collectors and sinners, people who sat loose to the law
in the most worldly manner.

As I write, I look up and out of the window. A tall
young man is coming along the pavement. He looks odd.
He is alone, but not wearing either the withdrawn or
the vaguely-interested-in-anything expression of those
who walk alone. He comes eagerly, with purposeful
steps, shoulders forward, cheerfully adjusting his coat
collar. My detective-novel training comes into play.
I deduce that he can see someone approaching still out
of my vision. I pause. I am not disappointed: it is a
charming girl. So that is why his attention was so fixed.

If we said that this young man had 'no eyes for anyone
else' we might be giving a fourth reason for a Christian's
indifference to the city—a desire not to be distracted. But
looking at the Father means looking at the world He
made for His joy; and turning your eyes upon Jesus
spotlights the faces of the hungry and the prisoner and
the stranger; and spotting the Holy Spirit takes you to the
goods yards of noisy life as well as the main lines of
through-devotion.

I can imagine the enthusiastic young man now gone
by suddenly receiving the full force of a pellet from a

small boy's pea-shooter; and when he high-mindedly
takes no notice and keeps his gaze on his beloved, she
shows her annoyance and says, 'Do look at him—I adore
small boys, especially cheeky ones.' God says to His city
saint, I am interested and involved in everything that
goes on in My world—so are you to be.

21

Friday

How are we to interpret the command to be separate?
It is certainly linked with the task of the Church in the
world. Elaborate methods were used in Israel for separat-
ing a priest for nearness to God in the conduct of ritual
worship. Prophets confronted the nation without institutional appointment, but they were expected to show the
signs. To make 'no difference' between holy and common,
and to say 'Thus saith the Lord' when the Lord had not
spoken, was a betrayal. Yet the priest was holy that the
nation might be holy, and the prophet was called to
effect national obedience.

The Church will betray the world she serves if she
conforms to it. But this has nothing to do with geographical position or physical separation at all. Religion has
its own forms of worldliness. Take three, and first pride.
The word 'Pharisee' also means 'separate' and was once
an honoured word. But the Pharisees made a fetish of
their exclusiveness and drew favourable comparisons
with lesser breeds. You and I will not cast the first stone.
Taking the moral life seriously is full of risk. The dilemma
begins in the nursery. When mother says, 'Johnny you
must wash your knees', how does she stop Johnny com-
paring his knees with Bobby's which are black with three
days' dirt? And if she says, 'You must not play with
boys with dirty knees', or even with pride, 'My boy

does not have dirty knees', what hope has Johnny then? For knees read character.

Then self-centredness. In personal terms we condemn this. How does the Church live? David Gourlay writes, 'The goal of the Church today is in itself. We have become a self-perpetuating organization of the most dangerous kind because we find divine sanctions for being as we are.' Is this what our forms of separation often produce?

Then indifference. We can separate ourselves for high matters, only to discover that Isaiah's definition of a fast is not to have more spiritual discipline than your neighbour, but to get entangled in the national fight against injustice; indeed, 'that thou hide not thyself from thine own flesh'.

We must take our notions of separation, as we took our ideas of holiness, from the nature of God. And we then see that the Church is to be separate, not in physical nor yet emotional terms, but in the quality of its life and purpose; just as God is separate, not by being distant in place or 'distant' in feeling, but in the holiness of His divine life and the purity of His purpose.

Then the Church is seen, not as lump, but as leaven; and the leaven must get to work in the lump. Christians are to be lights in the world; the reference, says D. T. Niles, is to street lights not sanctuary lights.

We see the Church working out exactly this role in the letter to Diognetus, dated late 2nd century: 'Though they live in Greek and barbarian cities, as each man's lot is cast, and follow the local customs in dress and food and the rest of their living, their own way of life which they display is wonderful and admittedly strange. They live in their native lands, but like foreigners. . . . They pass their days on earth, but they are citizens of heaven.

They obey the prescribed laws, and at the same time surpass the laws by their lives.'

And much more! The writer ends by saying that as the soul is in the body, so are Christians in the world. Compare this with our situation, in a secular world after centuries of Christendom. Christopher Dawson interprets our own day in this way: 'Men today are divided between those who have kept their spiritual roots and lost their contact with the existing order of society, and those who have preserved their social contacts and lost their spiritual roots.' Dr Alec Vidler sees this schism 'in the soul of modern man and in the souls of many Christian men', and asks whether the schism can be healed.

We must surely believe that it is on the way to being healed in the city saint whom we pursue. He, like the 'man of God' in 1 Tim 6, will shun the love of wrangling and the love of money. 'Shun' means 'flee from'—separate himself with the vigorous determination of a swift wing three-quarter evading the capture of clutching hands. By contrast, like a dogged fullback, he 'pursues' the Christian virtues. One of these is given as 'piety', which means the careful performance of devotional exercises. All the rest are 'in the world' virtues—not glasshouse, but common or garden. We shall look at some of them again. The first is righteousness, which has to do with a man's relationship with God and with man —or we should say, with God in man, and man in God. *The New English Bible* translates 'justice' to make it clear that it has everything to do with this world. The city saint's passion for justice will not allow him to be among the quiet of the land, who equate 'Christian' with 'keeping out of trouble'. There are missionary Churches which have given just that false impression, and we noticed the result of their influence at the beginning of this letter.

But I also remember a conversation with a Christian African city saint of conviction and maturity, who was—as some of his countrymen would have put it—wallowing in the political mire of his passionately divided country. When I tried to express appreciation of what he was doing and enduring, his quiet reply was, 'It's a job to be done'. Behind that unpretentious answer is the involvement of the 'holy nation' the Church in the world, through priestly act and prophetic word, and through the utmost participation. The Head of the Church is Incarnate God.

22

Saturday

P.S. The command to be separate and 'not to touch' is in Isa 52^{11}, quoted 2 Cor 6$^{14-18}$ (thought to be a fragment of an earlier letter than 1 Corinthians). Paul corrects the false impression in 1 Cor 5$^{9-13}$.

Christ's prayer is Jn 17^{15}. Gluttony comes in Prov 23^{20} and Mt 11^{19}, and leaven in Mt 13^{33}. The virtues of the 'man of God' are in 1 Tim 6^{11}.

The compromise of priest and prophet is Ezek 22$^{25-8}$, and Isaiah's fast is in chapter 58.

We shall be asking next time how the Church is to work out its involvement in the modern world. But I want now to share with you an experience I had a few weeks ago, which suggests another reason why the Church keeps apart; not because of its fear to compromise, but this time because it is lethargic and lacking in vision—in other words, because it is worldly.

I went to a public debate and looked for a city saint, alias 'knight of faith'. An alderman and a city councillor had gained a reputation for their opposition to the Campaign for Nuclear Disarmament, and had accepted the invitation of C.N.D. to debate the refusal of the City Council to allow 'peace corps'—C.N.D.-affiliated groups —in city schools. The standard of debate was low, partly because the Council members made no bones about their opinion that supporters of C.N.D. are misguided idiots, and partly because the great majority of the audience was made up of unimpressed and uninhibited supporters of the cause and the corps.

Through it all I looked for the city saint. Was he present? Was he the serious Training College student who said nothing, or the mother who had demonstrated for peace in Moscow, or the pleasant elderly clergyman who cheerfully chewed his way through the evening? Was he one of the well-dressed couple who spoke only to each other, or the young long-haired knight of the road with the silver cross dangling from one ear, rolled bed on his back, and a jacket-full of badges? Could it have been the anti-communist business man, or the angry school-teacher, or the idealistic schoolgirl, or the front-row scribbler whose scribbles were all handed up and torn up?

All my background was pushing me on to my feet, insisting that I say something, anything, so long as it began, 'As a Christian, I . . .' But I sat tight. I do not know in which book the angelic recorder registered a mark. I said nothing because whatever I said would probably have added up to this: 'Look here, at least one Christian is prepared to spend an evening on this subject, and to make his witness'. But that would have been making capital, as propagandists of all kinds do, out of the situation; and rightly suspect. I was a minister too involved in church life to 'know my stuff'; the facts and arguments presented made me feel a dabbler, an ignoramus.

And the Christian layman? I believe there may have

been a few incognito 'knights' present; but 60,000
church-goers had had the chance of seeing a large head-
line and a long column in the morning paper a day or
two earlier. Presumably some passed by on the other
column. Others may have said to themselves, 'If only I
were not at church four evenings this week, I might
possibly have gone if I could have found someone to go
with and if it hadn't been the evening I particularly hate
missing telly.' Others, perhaps, find controversial issues
disturbing, and to be avoided; others leave such matters
to our elected representatives; others only go to uplift
meetings.

Suppose we had all gone, all 60,000 of us? Leaving
aside the unelasticity of the shabby lecture room, and
the parking problems, what contribution would have been
made? How many of us really know the issues? Should
we have been content as long as the Church got a pat
on the back, and God was 'brought in'? As it happened,
God was only mentioned once in a question, and the
councillor in his reply clearly preferred to leave the
inscrutable purposes of God out of the discussion.

He was probably right. What matters in a debate
like this is not that God should have His honourable
mention, but that there should be in evidence the insights
and outlooks, the loving agony and the burning zeal,
which the Holy Spirit gives. Was not God's will and
grace involved in every opinion expressed and every
person expressing an opinion? Why if He is under and
through and in all things, should it be necessary to 'bring
Him in', as we say so significantly?

The city saint must be around, not to put in a word
for the Lord on every occasion (the Lord can look after
Himself), but to find Christ in what others have to contribute, and to contribute what Christ has given him.

But first he must be around.

Readings

You may like to take the following Readings for Mothering Sunday:

Ecclus 38$^{24-34}$ The city worker

Gal 4$^{21-8}$ The freedom of Jerusalem 'our mother'

Lk 19$^{1-10}$ Citizen of Jericho

Holy Calling

'called us to a dedicated life'

23

Monday

Dear Joe,

You must 'be around', just because you belong to God's people, separated and set free to get His will done in every city circumstance. Christ the man is involved in the life of all men through His Body the Church. You are a member of the Body. But as a layman you do not need to make strenuous efforts to go into the world. You are already there.

But are you—forgive the question—*all* there? Much has been said in recent years about the ecclesiastical layman who is so enmeshed in the intricate machinery of church institutional life that his daily secular work and responsibilities become for him a regrettable interruption. To some Jesus said and says, Leave what you are doing and follow Me by doing something else. To others He said and says, Go home, Stay put. Matthew leaves his tax duties—and it is one kind of absurdity that a man making money hand over fist should prefer another kind of life. Zacchaeus continues his work—and it is another kind of absurdity that he should have done so with an attitude of fair and honest dealing.

A young man said to me recently, 'Since I was converted my work means less and less to me.' We will not

blame him. For many there is a stage in the pilgrimage
of faith when 'the things of earth' grow strangely dim.
You may see why if you think of your wife. I rather think
that in the days when you were finding out that she was
'right' for you, you also felt a slackening in your interest
in music and cricket and even the sea. You were all
wrapped up in her. And then you both realized that
healthy courtship is enjoying things together, not just
enjoying one another; not only looking into each other's
eyes, but turning two pairs of eyes in the same interesting
direction. So in healthy spiritual development the time
must come when the 'strangely dim' is replaced by
'wonderfully bright'. As George Wade Robinson expressed it:

> 'Something lives in every hue
> Christless eyes have never seen.'

The whole world of experience takes on a new look for
the city saint.

Including work. More and more discussion is taking
place—and needs to take place—about being a Christian
in industry. People speak sometimes as though four
years theological training, degrees in economics and
sociology, and a life-time's activity in management or
trade union methods, were the minimum requirement;
whereas nothing must close our eyes to the working
Christian's first duty to live fully in the work he does and
the place where he does it. Look again at Kierkegaard's
'knight': 'He does his job thoroughly. At first glance
you would think he was a clerk who had lost his soul to
double-entry book-keeping, so punctilious he is.'

Our saint is to give his best undivided attention to the
job in hand; to do what he is paid to do cheerfully and
conscientiously; to view the work of himself and others

in terms of contribution to the life of the city and the world; to recognize that to be involved in structures of society not yet conforming to the 'pattern on the mountain' must inevitably mean some tension and some compromise—and therefore honesty with himself and his fellows; to do what thinking he can about how Christ is to be proclaimed Lord of the expanding economy and the limited company; and to obey Him with the best insights he can develop. His work—far from being a necessary evil, or a nagging nuisance, or a second-best to full-time labour in the Church, or a marking-time between the marches of dedicated living—will be an important and immediate sphere of service to God. And he will be working out, sometimes with effort, sometimes with exhilaration, what Christ-calledness, Christ-likeness, and Christ-usefulness (all essential marks of holiness) mean in terms of daily labour. Those virtues of the 'man of God' mentioned in 1 Tim 6, for example, are disturbingly relevant to the office and the factory floor. Look at 'patience' and 'meekness' (RV). They sound only fit for the stained-glass-window saint. But NEB has 'fortitude and gentleness', which brings us a little nearer. The lectionary takes us all the way: the one Greek word meaning 'strong and reliable', which could be found on any factory notice-board advertising vacancies; and the other 'treating others with respect', a quality that does not go unnoticed in any office in the country. We could translate 'firm and considerate', and trace both words in the comment of a 'junior' girl about the woman in charge of her section: 'She is always there and she doesn't forget that I'm here.'

Another word in the catalogue, 'piety' (RV—godliness), should remind the city saint that throughout his working life he continues to be a member of the Church—the Church dispersed in the world. With the Church as his

Mother, he will know the security that enables a man to go out in freedom to join those of whom Scripture says, 'Without these shall not a city be inhabited'.

24

Tuesday

A statement from the World Council of Churches asks for a deeper understanding of 'Stewardship' in the Church, and says, 'It should not be narrowly confined but should be seen in the light of total dedication of one's gifts to the glory of God in all spheres of life'. Daily work is mentioned, and much is made of the fact that many of the services once begun and carried out by Churches have been taken over by government and secular service agencies. Certainly in health and education, social welfare and youth work, Christians have great possibilities and obligations in our day. It is suggested that they can, because of their faith and outlook, turn 'what might be impersonal service into truly personal service through a consciousness of the saving presence of Christ'.

The city saint is also involved in the needs of the community through leisure-time activity. Unless he and many like him are prepared to make themselves available to people in special need, many in the city will be neglected and the wide needs of people throughout the world unmet. He may do this within voluntary organizations, or in less formal ways. With increased leisure, and the promise of much more to come, city people have a growing responsibility for one another and those beyond its boundaries. Telly, and other more sociable activities, can mean an extensive waste of time which could often be put to better—and happier—use. How many hours, and what sorts of programmes, do you allow yourself for eye-exercise? How many for tongue-exercise? And do you sometimes go to bed remembering someone who would really have welcomed a visit and now must wait?

But service itself can become a bad habit, an absorbing fanaticism, an alibi for living. The city saint must 'religiously' keep leisure for his family and friends; for the enjoyment of a world of beauty and fascination which God has pronounced good; for increasing his knowledge of gulls or galaxies, mountains or molecules; for the results of man's use of his creative powers, in art and music, ballet and poetry, which show him to be made in the image of his Maker.

He will be interested in all that goes on—more, not less, than the man at the next bench. If he is not interested in racing, he will not pretend he is. If he hates football and is bored with cricket, he will neither hide the fact nor parade it. He will cultivate such interests as he has, even if the time he can conscientiously give is very limited. He will be open to catch and appreciate the enthusiasms of others, not resenting the fact that healthy-minded people get absorbed in fishing and model aeroplanes, dogs and horses, pigeon-fancying and ballroom dancing, and refuse to get morbid about their sins.

He will try to understand those whom T. S. Eliot called 'decent, godless people', whose attitude to sex or swearing, drink or bingo, may be different from his own. When he sees suffering caused by the denial of love and duty, he may have to speak out and be unpopular; and he will know that the guilty as well as the innocent have feelings and that the combinations of guilt and innocence are—outside popular novels and films—kaleidoscopic. He will not be shocked, for he has learnt from Christ and his experience what is in man; including himself. He knows that by living in the city, with its rates and taxes and votes and corporate life, he is involved in the decisions of local and national government and must know something about the Rent Act, and the financial needs of cancer research, and the effects of raising the school-leaving age, and the duty of western people in a world of lavish plenty and hungry poverty.

The city saint will consider all these things from a theological angle, and experience them on the 'Godward' and on the 'manward' side. He will know that as early as New Testament days, and often since, people have thought they were doing God a service by calling the world of matter evil, and denying anything good to the 'flesh'. He will recognize that the world is rebellious—but God made it for Himself; and that the flesh is weak—but God gave it for a good purpose. At the centre of his awareness will be 'Jesus Christ come in the flesh', and a world that is not only the sphere of the activity of evil, but also the stuff of Christ's presence and victory.

In this conviction he will 'be around', not just by unavoidable necessity or hard choice, but as one who, within the representative priesthood of the Church, is privileged to share with his Lord the agony and the glory. And because of these things, it will be said of the city saint by those who understand, 'He is a splendid follower of Christ—he never misses Panorama'. Or 'He is a most devout man—he may forget his prayers occasionally but he always reads the morning paper'. Or perhaps, 'She lives a dedicated life—look at the trouble she takes over her cooking'. Or again, 'Since his conversion he has got to know more about industrial disputes than any man in the factory'. Or even, 'She has the makings of a saint—she is never on church premises except on Sundays'.

25

Wednesday

P.S. 'Called to a dedicated life' is 2 Tim 1^9, NEB. The RV has 'called us with a holy calling'. St Paul's exposition of the Body of Christ is in 1 Cor 12^{12-27}. The different ways Jesus dealt with people is seen in Lk 5^{10-11} and 8^{39}; also in Lk 19^{1-10} (Zacchaeus) and Mt 9^9 (Matthew). The hymn mentioned is 'Loved with everlasting love' MHB 443.

A moving passage in Ecclesiasticus (in the Apocrypha) Chapter 38 speaks of the scribe and compares him with the artisans, who are described in these terms:

'Without these shall not a city be inhabited,
And men shall not sojourn nor walk up and down therein.
They shall not be sought for in the council of the people . . .
But they will maintain the fabric of the world;
And in the handiwork of their craft is their prayer.'

Modern industrial man may like to study the ideas of craft guilds of centuries before the Industrial Revolution. The emphasis was on standards of workmanship and protection and fair dealing for all concerned. Along similar lines we hear in the 17th century of a Tailors' Brotherhood founded in Paris by a Roman Catholic layman named Buch from Luxemburg. The purpose was spiritual upbuilding 'by the practice of the love of God in the exercise of their craft, of fellowship with their equals, of fidelity towards their neighbours in work and in business, and of watchfulness in dealing with the world in such a way as not to be touched by the corruption which is inseparable from it'. This is quoted on one of the 408 pages (p. 310) of the fascinating historical symposium, *The Layman in Christian History*, published by the World Council of Churches 1963.

The quotation from the World Council of Churches is from *New Delhi Speaks*; p. 50. The Bishop of Coventry was recently reported on radio and in the newspapers as having spoken of the Church as often looking like a collection of like-minded 'Holy Joes'. This kind of thing is 'news', but the Church must not mind truth being spoken about itself publicly, nor let it go unheeded. It would appear that what the Bishop was advocating was much more interest by Christian people in the arts.

One protest against the idea that matter is evil, and therefore marriage and meat highly suspect, is in 1 Tim 4^{1-5}. The emphasis that Jesus Christ is come in the flesh is in 1 Jn 4^{1-3}.

We turn to prayer—based on Jn 12^{44-50}, NEB.

Intercessions

Read Jn 12^{44-6}

O Christ, eternal Light, who—sent by the Father— hast sent the Church into the world to convey light; may Thy people, involved in the advances of science and the atmosphere of modern thought, reflect Thy truth and grace; that men, seeing their life and witness, may believe in Thee, and seeing Thy glory embodied, may see the Father.
Silence.

Read Jn 12^{47-8}

O Christ, appointed by the Father as Judge of all, who didst come into the world to preach peace and to bring a sword; may Thy people, involved in a world at war with itself, be open to Thy judgment; that men, desiring

peace but rejecting its conditions, may be pointed to
Thee, and hearing Thy word may be made whole.
Silence.

Read Jn 12⁴⁹⁻⁵⁰
O Christ, Word of the Father, who hast made known to
us by the Holy Spirit the divine will of perfect love;
may Thy people, involved in the upheaval of technological
change in city and country, know what to say and how to
speak; that men, hearing the word of new life proclaimed
with authority, may obey Thy commands, and know
in experience that the darkness is passing and the real
light already shines.
Silence.

Holy Mission

'and the city shall have suburbs'

26

Thursday

Dear Joe,

To be a member of the 'scattered' Church is to be involved in the life of the city in work and leisure. But the Church is also 'gathered', with a local habitation and a name, bearing a particular responsibility towards the neighbourhood where it finds itself and the city as a whole.

It is gathered in Sunday worship; especially in Holy Communion when Mother Church brings her children together to the warmth of the family table. In addition to regular worship, the city saint will need opportunities of closer fellowship in the small group—which will only be healthy if it is looking beyond fellowship. He will need training in the faith and its city and universal outworking. And he will also, as far as other essential involvement makes it possible, be available for witness and service within the organized life of the Church.

This is not as simple as it sounds, for the modern city is a large and complicated structure. I was recently shocked by a verse in Ezekiel describing the ideal Jerusalem: 'And the city shall have suburbs: toward the north two hundred and fifty and toward the south two hundred and fifty, and toward the east . . .' It sounded exactly like the sprawling conurbation in which I live. Then I found that the figures refer not to suburbs but to cubits —measurements of length. A modern translation completed my disillusionment. 'Suburb' is translated 'open land' and it becomes clear that in this city the people live in the central areas, and the 'portions' for general use are round the outskirts. That is what my city used to be like, as witness the number of teeming suburbs still named 'Heath'; and there are still parks. But the city is now the reverse of Ezekiel's: the suburbs are residential and the centre with its shops, offices, law-courts, cafés, is shared by all.

This means that the city saint will probably live in one place (if fortunate like you, in a pleasant suburb), work in another, in the inner industrial areas or far out, and have contact with the city centre through central meetings, theatres and clubs, shopping and eating out. His unsettledness and mobility may cause him to worship in a church that is not in any of these places. He may choose a church where the worship, the atmosphere, the theology of the sermons and the colour of the carpets, are congenial to him. What do we say to that? He can express his Christian faith anywhere, and if he is young and impressionable, he must get nourishing spiritual food somewhere. He will, however, not allow himself to settle down in easy surroundings for the rest of his life; he will keep alert to the fact that warm likemindedness and Christian fellowship are not at all the same thing; and he will be mindful of neighbourhood, tough-area, and total city needs.

Most Christians will find their sphere of organized Church activity in their own neighbourhood. Stewardship will express itself in the tasks of the local Church; training others, as teacher of children or leader of house

fellowship; serving others by contacts within and beyond
Church boundaries; supporting the institutional life of the
Church by planned giving and humble chores; and repre-
senting the Church in the manifold life of suburb and city.

The city saint will not be content for the local Church
to make the odd contact here and do the occasional job
there. He will want the Church to engage in outreach,
with system in it, arising from a sense of responsibility
for the whole area. This is hardly possible without full
co-operation between the Churches 'in one place'. The
anomalies of independently run denominational centres
going about their own business are only hidden while
none of them is making any significant contribution to
the neighbourhood. If all were visiting frequently,
and engaged in local, educational and community
activities, it would be an impossible situation and something would be done. Further, local divisions make
Christ's Church look more like a series of holy huddles
than a representative priesthood.

There is a growing number of experiments in unity, on
the lines described in *Responsibility in the Welfare State*. In
'Southbridge', a fictitious name but a genuine Birmingham
suburb, the Council of Churches employed professional
sociologists to survey the area. It was discovered that one
family in five had a clear need which the welfare state
was not meeting. Much light was thrown on the attitude
of residents—such as the woman who said she would like
to go to church but knew she would give the impression
to her neighbours that she wanted to be a cut above them.
As a result of this investigation, Church leaders began to
meet regularly with those working for various statutory
and voluntary welfare organizations, and Church
members made themselves available to provide help. This
particular scheme has been encountering rough water
through denominational changes in leadership.

Another suburban area has seen the five Protestant Churches combine in the provision of Parish Stewards for every street. There is good liaison, close co-operation with welfare services, and the expressed aim that 'no need goes unnoticed'.

It has been astonishing to find how much human need there is in 'prosperous' suburbs, and the city saint will participate in Church activity as he can. He will do so realizing that there are other areas of the city where the need is wide and desperate.

27

Friday

The 'twilight' areas of the city are so called because they are on the edge of redevelopment areas, not quite 'black' enough to be included in city rebuilding schemes. The name has also been linked with the mixture of immigrants and others who are part of the multi-racial urban society. The city has other inner areas undergoing the strains of rebuilding and large-scale movement of population; and others which will mark time for twenty years before the tide of demolition sweeps them away.

In Churches still hanging on uncertainly in these parts, the only stability is often provided by people who live right outside and are unaffected by changes. And where large-scale building has already taken place there are very few flat-dwellers to provide the Church nucleus. All these are missionary areas, and must be treated as such by the whole Church. The best chance of the Church is often to be linked up with other Churches within such a framework as a Methodist Circuit. The strains and challenges of such a situation can be immense; but this is genuine Christian sharing over boundaries of class and culture.

Some city saints must be gladly spared from their own place to come and identify themselves completely with these areas. They will come in the modern missionary spirit, aware that this is a special call within the total need of Church and city. They will ponder all the objectionable sides to missionary activities across boundaries. They will come humbly, prepared, in fellowship, knowing that they must constantly be on the lookout for local people to do the jobs and take the responsibilities.

There is a need for some to live in the neighbourhood. Some Methodist university students are beginning to do so after college. Practical problems abound, but you should read Bruce Kenrick's *Come Out the Wilderness* to see what becomes possible through genuine, concentrated participation in a neighbourhood. Many inner-belt Churches have been struggling towards death for years, and most remedies have been shown up as superficial. There is a cost to count, if mission is to become possible.

The need for united effort in such places should be obvious enough. A few months ago one inner area of this city received the full glare of press publicity. The houses were due for demolition within three years, and many had been occupied by problem families. Through the initiative of city dignitaries and Christian people in the neighbourhood a Residents' Association was formed. Anglicans, Roman Catholics, and Methodists co-operated, and the chairman was provided by Rotary. The city saint will learn in such situations to put need before vested interests, however religious.

Inside the inner residential neighbourhoods the city central areas will provide facilities for administration, recreation, and a wide variety of general interests. The city saint will see himself as part of a total city witness, and may therefore have some links with a central urban church.

The value of central churches and central halls is still under discussion. It must be recognized that surburban church life has its limitations. It is inevitably linked with leisure hours when men and women are away from the heat and burden of the working day. This has sometimes meant that people have wanted the Church to be a withdrawal from the hard facts of life; and sometimes that leaders have been far less business-like in their church lives than in their business lives. The city saint will resist these temptations.

Suburban church life can indeed help those living under tolerable worries and intolerable strains; it can also minister to family life and to neighbourhood needs. But the Christian message is for the whole of life, and needs its expression where people work and play, and where significant events and decisions take place. A city church will have a very different 'look' from a neighbourhood church. It should.

Some Christians will want to identify themselves and their families with the central church, realizing its special needs and the peculiar inconveniences and problems that arise for those involved. This witnessing society has special openings for friendship and care, contact and witness, especially among those who in various ways are unsettled. It will speak best to the city's needs through the closest co-operation with other Christians in the centre.

The suburban Church member should have some contact with the central church. He may take advantage of training which is provided for all sharing in city life: a Saturday training school, a monthly study group on industrial society, or better still a winter's course of lectures towards the understanding of God and God's world.

He will support and take advantage of the specialized full-time ministries focussed at the centre—the work of chaplains connected with hospitals, factories, stores colleges, forces, or prison; hostels making special provision for those needing care; and activities connected with immigrants, or family and social welfare, or youth and age. His local Church will benefit from these services, and be challenged to participate in wide mission to city people. Centrally recognized needs must be linked with willing suburban Christians. He may come forward to help in counselling, open-air witness, or industrial consultations. He will probably share not only in local house fellowships with a strong 'frontier' emphasis, but also in central groups made up of people of the same profession or interest.

Amid all these multitudinous opportunities, the city saint will discriminate and offer his particular contribution among the Church's diversities of gifts. He will undoubtedly have to face misunderstanding and criticism towards himself, and hesitancy and opposition towards new plans and methods. He will press all the Churches to discover together a total strategy. He will do what he can that the Church may be set forth, in architecture and structure, mission and ministry, as the Servant of the city —the city whose name may yet become 'The Lord is there'.

28

Saturday

P.S. The Ezekiel passage is chapter 48. Note particularly verses 17 and 35. The anomalies of Churches of different denominations exercising their priestly ministry in the same neighbourhood were certainly in mind when the World Council of Churches drew up its statement on 'The Unity We Seek'. You may not have seen it, Joe, or have forgotten it. It deserves, and is still getting, a great deal of attention. You will find it in many publications of the British Council of Churches, and in particular in every one of the 'Faith and Order' series of booklets entitled 'The Unity We Seek'.

Responsibility in the Welfare State is published at 5s. by the Birmingham Council of Christian Churches. I will gladly send you a copy. It is a well-presented sociological report, and has received considerable publicity in several countries.

In the other suburb I mentioned, a special Service was held for the commissioning of Parish Stewards. The statement read during the Service said, 'Those being commissioned are officially to represent the Church in their road, and to be the channels through which help may be given to those in need, that all may know that the Church does care for them.' Then the Stewards were addressed: 'You are to carry out a vital part of the Church's work by making certain, as far as lies in your power, that no need goes unnoticed.'

Later, in the commissioning itself, the purpose was stated as follows: 'that the Church may become a more effective agent in spreading Christ's love throughout this neighbourhood'. Then all present at the Service, representing the five denominational Churches, were reminded 'that they have been set apart to do this service for you and their Lord. They are your brethren and God's fellow-workers.'

An American professor, Dr Gibson Winter, argues strongly for the linking of outer and inner suburban Churches in *The Surban Captivity of the Churches*. The title is fair warning of his drastic criticism of the respectable Church in suburbia. In a more recent book, difficult but dynamic, *The New Creation as Metropolis*, he sees the city Church radically different in structure from usual forms of Church life, but in every essential way 'the Church'—with immense possibilities in training and communication.

What do you think I meant, Joe, by the objectionable sides to missionary activity? You will find that annual reports of Missionary Societies give very valuable clues to the attitude and methods required in a missionary situation: that is, when 'natural' boundaries are crossed in order to share the Good News. You certainly must read Bruce Kenrick's book, which describes the way new openings developed in New York's worst slum area, East Harlem. The 'price' included families committing themselves to live in the area, community living, unconventional ways, many failures, endless training and consultation, wide support—including grants from central funds, and complete ecumenical unity.

The area with the Residents' Association is being written up by a colleague of mine, Rev. Joseph Rimmer, and I hope you will soon be able to read his report of what is happening. There is much to be learnt from these new, sometimes carefully planned, sometimes unexpected, developments.

Canon Boulard, a Roman Catholic priest and sociologist, has some deeply significant things to say about the mission of the Church in *An Introduction to Religious Sociology*, 1960 (Darton, Longman and Todd). He stresses the participation of modern man in various groups, and the necessity for the Church to work out its task within those groups. One outcome is the study group of men of the same profession, helping one another sort out their common responsibilities and resources.

As for hesitancy and opposition, we sometimes envy the fresh approaches taking place in the United States. But

Dr Howard Grimes of Dallas comments, 'Protestantism has generally been reluctant to discard conventional forms of congregational life, even in those areas of both country and city where the Church is badly failing.' He says of the city that creative work has been done on a small scale through the 'large parish'—the joining of several small congregations into one. The Paul Report about the Church of England makes suggestions along these lines. Dr Grimes adds, 'Not much has occurred of a significant nature by way of the renewal of the church in the inner city.'

An indication of both present inertia and urge for re-thinking is found in the Haynes' Report—the report of a committee appointed by the Boys' Brigade to look into its present aim and work. The Report asks 'Can the Brigade be Church-anchored without being Church-centred?' The B.B. knows the need for radical change, and the difficulty of being tied to an organization strongly resistant to change. The *British Weekly* comments, 'If the B.B. movement can create that true layman whose Christian "witness" is not in Church-centred activities, but in the key structures of society where they live, work, play, it will render a notable service to the Church.'

Readings

Readings for Passion Sunday:

Isa 52⁺³–53¹²   God's Suffering Servant
Heb 5¹⁻¹⁰, 7²⁶⁻⁸   Suffering and priesthood
Mt 25³¹⁻⁴⁶   The relief of suffering

Holy Time

'use the present opportunity to the full'

29

Monday

Dear Joe,

It was all very well for Wordsworth to enjoy so much working leisure 'away from it all'. You remember—

> 'It was a beauteous evening, calm and still,
> The holy time was quiet as a nun
> Breathless with adoration.'

But 7 a.m. brings the dash to work, and concentrated work is punctured with interruptions, and dull work is punctuated with music, and the lunch break is cut short to make 'more time' later, and 5 p.m. is the rush hour, and evenings are never long enough, and the best telly programmes are late, and to get to the country is too much effort after a day's work, and at the weekend everybody else has the same idea, and when we get to management level we have the worry as well as the work. . . . When were you last calm and still?

In such a world the city saint is to let his ordered life confess the beauty of God's peace. It takes some doing. And in my last two letters I have been piling on the unrelenting responsibility of every member of the 'holy priesthood', the claim to work and leisure time, the opening up of a thousand duties and opportunites of which nine hundred and ninety-five must remain a dream.

We sometimes grumble that Churches are tranquil, but most city Churches lay on the layman more and more jobs, or more and more bouts of conscience for not doing them, until the ungodly hours are breathless with exertion. You think I exaggerate? I hope I do. Somehow in all this there must be balance and discernment. Somehow the Holy Spirit must help us create order. Somehow we must accept a heavier burden than activities —that of being a certain sort of person. Otherwise we may start thinking we are justified by deeds done and distance covered. We may become well-doers-on-strings, and—wanting to give ourselves to people—find there is little of ourselves to give; our manner restless, our time short, our interests small, our company boring, our insights clouded, our energies dissipated, and our attitude idolatrous because we have come to believe that it *all* depends on us.

I was talking recently to a mature city layman about the pattern of life that he had come to adopt. Because of small children he and his wife manage to go to church together three or four times a year. At other times they take it in turns in the evenings, and he always goes in the mornings. He thoughtfully and humbly accepts the leadership of worship from minister or local preacher, and avoids being over-critical by asking himself, 'What is this man's forte—conduct of worship, preaching, or something quite different?' (I mention this in passing as a particular mark of holiness!) His own contribution is through systematic giving, choir membership, and Sunday School teaching. He has also accepted special responsibilities in the circuit, and in connexion with a city church. He reckons to be on church premises at least three nights a week.

His contact with people outside Church life is through his work. He runs a social club which meets mainly in the lunch break. He used to play football. He keeps in touch with non-churchgoing friends. He does not go to pubs, and finds it difficult to endure parties where 'what's to drink looms larger than what's to do'. His social work mainly consists in helping with an annual door-to-door collection.

Here is a good pattern, familiar and necessary, the stuff of active church life. I mention it so that you may analyse yours. How church-centred is it becoming? What you must avoid, Joe, is the piecemeal addition of things, without reference to the principle of priesthood. God calls us to action through a casual contact, or a chance circumstance; He will also help us with the full picture. Kierkegaard says of his knight, 'The whole earthly shape which he assumes is something newly created by virtue of the absurd. In his infinite resignation he gave up everything and then regained everything by virtue of the absurd.' The absurdity of the Cross and Passion alone makes sense of the form of consecrated living in the world.

Four things occur to me about this 'earthly shape'. First, every detail is ultimately justified by its service to God in the world. The priestly ministry is for the sake of those who do not yet share it.

Secondly, every man and woman must find the appropriate pattern. Each has his own. Yet one must help another. Never mind about others, Joe. Think of yourself. Perhaps you will only discover what holiness implies for you as you talk it over frankly with somebody else equally desiring to understand and to live the holy life in 1980 terms (it being good to keep a little ahead of the times). It is all the better when married couples can

thrash out together the practical outworking of their
stewardship. And you may also look to the experienced
help of a 'spiritual adviser'—once you have found the
right person.

Thirdly, you will need to settle the difference in use of
Sunday and weekdays. It could be that for many at
present Sunday is a sad waste of 'the present opportunity'.

And last, you will need to work out the place of prayer.
To this we turn.

30

Tuesday

Honest to God helped many who were going about with
a bad conscience, accepting that they ought to pray
regularly, yet somehow never managing it and finding
little reality in it when they did. Yet there are city saints
who, even amid the bustle of these days, know the value
of a disciplined prayer life. Others are convinced they
need it, and know how much is lost when they lose it.

If we are to 'pray without ceasing', that is in life, why is
prayer at a particular time necessary? It could be an
escape tunnel, a funk-hole. Let us try to discover what
prayer is. The holy life is communion with God, in every
part, awake or asleep, active or passive, for ever broken
and for ever renewed. Then we could think of prayer as
the conscious moments of communion with God—except
that many of us find with the Bishop of Woolwich that
we can often be less aware of God during 'times of prayer'
than in the heat of the day's life. Should I say then that
prayer means those times when I am aware that life is
communion with God? That will not do, because prayer
is not just reflexion, but part of a dynamic relationship.

Let us put it this way: Prayer is the conscious recogni-

tion of God's holy presence and purpose in all life—
including the 'now' of prayer. This, as we saw when
we thought about worship, will usually involve the use
of words. We have the words of Scripture to convey
God's meaning in events; we are to make a meaningful
reply, using words to communicate, to clarify, to commit
ourselves.

That makes prayer engagement, as well as withdrawal.
Prayer should no more be remote from life than life itself.
Mature life has a balance of activity and passivity, of
giving out and taking in, of rush and rest. Prayer, for
all its physical inactivity, is to be seen on both sides of
the scales. For a man's inner life is as complex as his
outer life, and prayer is private life facing Godwards, as
worship is public life facing Godwards.

Prayer, as life, needs its pattern; here too, we can help
one another; and here too, the pattern will emerge
from the 'priesthood'—from our lively contact with God
and our world. In Pasternak's *Dr Zhivago*, Lara went to
church because 'she needed the accompaniment of an
inward music, and she could not always compose it for
herself'. Liturgy informs prayer. But so does life. Equally
needed is the discordant clamour of the secular world.
Prayer is the contrapuntal combination of two not
entirely dissimilar melodies—God's holiness and God's
world.

If we look at the various elements of prayer, we find
that all prayer is about God and about the life of an
estranged world. Christian prayer always expresses
'God's life in us for the world'. The recommended
methods of meditation show this. In that which goes
with the name of St Ignatius of Loyola, the one who
prays takes a passage of Scripture and looks for God's
contemporary Word in it. He begins with what is

sometimes called 'remote preparation', defined as 'the firm resolve to live the life of Christian holiness'. He ends with a practical resolution. This is anything but a holy daydream; its interest is obedience in the world.

Contemplative meditation is also worth your attention. In it we relax body and mind to a state of quiet receptivity. In the silence we hold in our thoughts a word of God which is personal, and immediate; something we believe with the top of our heads, but which has not yet fully penetrated and cleansed the depths of our minds. Three minutes at a time is enough; the aim—to be an integrated person, to be centrally still, to be Christ-like, to be what the world needs me to be.

Take more familiar kinds of prayer. The world is still in evidence. Affirmation—so important in all our praying —is the statement that God has centred the world in Christ crucified, for His glory and its sanctification. What we ask for in petition has to do with our life and calling in the world. Thanksgiving covers exactly the same ground —and intercession, with others in mind. Our usual confessions often lack the 'music' of God's promise and the world's sin. But our most private sins have connotations far wider than we realize, and special links with our vocation as 'priests'. In Graham Greene's *The Power and the Glory* the Mexican whiskey-priest makes his confession before execution, and as he prays forgiveness with an illegitimate daughter in mind, he knows that all his love is focussed upon her, and he knows that is the love he should have discovered towards every one of those for whom he has some responsibility.

Adoration is also about life. To say 'Blessed be God' can cost nothing. To back the currency of praise with the gold of obedience costs life; life given in Christ for God's sake and the world's.

Once more we find a sharp pointer in the 'knight of faith'. Kierkegaard says that the most difficult feat that a ballet dancer can attempt is to jump and take a definite attitude without faltering. If I interpret him right, he is saying that both life's experiences and prayer can be like that jump upward. But his comment is, 'To be able to transform the leap into life into a normal gait, to be able to express perfectly the sublime in terms of the pedestrian —only the knight can do this—and this is the single miracle.' Prayer equips us to be God's secular men. This way, the 'holy time' may be as quiet as a nun or as noisy as the city's indoor market, yet the rhythmic breathing in and breathing out of the saint's 'sound pair of lungs' will together serve one purpose—the adoration of God, through service to the world.

31

Wednesday

P.S. The Scriptural quotation is from Col 4^{2-6}. AV has 'redeeming the time'. The hymn quoted is MHB 669.

The Methodist 'Renewal Group' takes seriously the need for mutual help in seeking the pattern of holiness. The Rule says, 'Accepting our personal need of renewal and order, each of us is obliged to work out, preferably with another person, what his "rule" should be. . . . This obligation has wide references. Many members live the family life and their rule involves others. So wherever possible a member of the Group and wife (or husband) should consult with another family linked with the Group. The initial need is for each person or family to discover the appropriate personal rule for them. This should be followed regularly by meetings with another member or family, to consider their rules, how they have been kept, and what revision follows experience. Such

conversation may lead to confession and the mutual
assurance of God's forgiveness and restoration. Some
members may desire to ask a qualified person to become
their spiritual advisor.' Three matters are then especially
mentioned, personal and family stewardship, ministry,
and a pattern and habit of devotional life. As a member
of this Group I must add that some members are hesitant
about rules and habits, and there is no obligation except
that mentioned at the beginning of the quotation. A man
may decide that his rule must be not to have a rule.

One of many fine examples of the giving of spiritual
help mentioned in *The Layman in Christian History*, is
Madame de Swetchine. She was a Russian Roman
Catholic lay woman, who kept open house in Paris in
the years 1836–48 and received the most distinguished
representatives of political, legal, and artistic life. One
leader of Catholic renewal said she kept him from loss
of courage and enthusiasm, and when she died Augustin
Cochin spoke of the depth of the impression left upon
him 'by that holy woman, who so fully brought to realiza-
tion the miracle of holiness in the midst of the world'.

When the city saint has begun to work out his own
pattern, he may find trouble. Yesterday I met for the
first time in years a young layman who in college was
a keen, thoughtful and lively Christian. Now he teaches
physics, and is deeply concerned to serve God in his work.
But he is very discouraged. He has a family, he preaches,
he runs the church youth club against agonizing non-
cooperation, and apparently nobody thinks he is pulling
his weight in Church life—mainly because he has said
No to taking a Sunday School class.

You must think more about this use of Sunday. I will
make just one negative and one positive observation.
I could not expect you to attend two Services with

exactly the same form on a Sunday; and if I were a layman I should want a weekly service of Word and Sacrament, and the chance of using Sunday for the training I needed, to leave me free to be out and about more during the week.

You should read the chapter on prayer in *Honest to God* if you are one of the ten people in Europe who have not done so. It is interesting that Bonhoeffer, so often quoted by Robinson, put much stress on a disciplined prayer life, and practised it.

Of course prayer can be an escape, and sometimes is. We find Erasmus saying in the 16th century that a ruler who spends his time in prayer instead of properly administering the affairs of his subjects is no true Christian. You and I, Joe, are seldom in this kind of danger, except perhaps when we try to make up the lack of a prayer-time when driving a car.

I mentioned the Bible in connexion with our devotions. I leave you to work out the advantages and disadvantages of reading the Bible daily. I am quite sure every Christian must read the Bible for himself, and study it with a commentary. And this means time—even if not daily.

You will draw much on the Bible, probably a modern version, to help with your pattern of daily prayer. I think you should have a 'skeleton' for morning and evening, and you can then find biblical passages and other people's prayers as well as your own to fill in the flesh. I suggest the following for morning: Silence, Invitation to come, Short Confession, Psalm and Ascription of Praise, Lesson and quiet meditation, Prayer of offering, Blessing. And for evening: Silence, Invitation, Confession (with the day in mind), Affirmation (such as an ancient hymn), Supplication (prayer for self and others), Blessing.

You will find details of the kind of meditation I mentioned in W. L. Knox, *Meditation and Mental Prayer*, SPCK, 1960; and for Contemplative Meditation see the writings of M. V. Dunlop, obtainable from the Fellowship of Meditation, 3, Longdown, Guildford.

The quotation from Kierkegaard is very close in thought to the observation of A. N. Whitehead: 'That religion will conquer which can render clear to popular understanding some eternal greatness incarnate in the passage of temporal fact.'

And finally John Wesley's prayer: 'Cure us of this intermitting piety, and fix it into an even and a constant holiness.'

Holy Place

'the priests stood in their place'

32

Thursday

Dear Joe,

Have you spotted him yet—this elusive pimpernel hiding among the gay and gray colours of city life? We have been searching for him through the eyes of others— biblical writers, Kierkegaard, contemporary men of insight. Do we see him with our own eyes?

There he is in the crowd. Over to the right—for he knows the city has been given much good to conserve. Now a bit to the left—for he questions everything, even the solid structures of men's life together and his own surest beliefs. He is difficult to pick out; is not as tall as I thought; stands well-balanced yet poised for movement; has strong, sensitive hands and alert eyes; manages most of the time to avoid treading on other people's toes; yet has a strong pair of elbows to prevent himself being shoved or squashed.

It would be impossible to describe his clothes and appearance. For although in other times and places saints have been mainly of one social class, or one custom of life, or similar dress or habits or language, modern saints reflect the diversity of their society, and show astonishing variations from country to country, city to city, street to street, house to house. But whether a

somebody or a nonentity, man or woman, whatever
age or income group or intelligence, what do we know
for certain about the place of this person in the world?

This city saint was called by God to be human and holy,
to find in a priestly-prophetic community a share in
Christ's prayer and deed for the world, to live a Spirit-
guided life of a new quality, working it out in the stuff
of city living and the fabric of corporate ministry, learning
how to leap into the awareness of the Godward side of
things so as to land assuming a 'normal gait'.

His eyes will not be towards heaven as he carves the
joint; and in the garden he is more likely to be thinking
of the heart of the lettuce than God's heart; nor will he
have a text—nor even an answer—to every problem. Yet
he senses in all things a providence, and breathes a purer
air even in the city atmosphere.

He knows his place. His place is where Christ is, seated
at the right hand of God, seated by a flabby woman at a
well; at Christ's side in the midst of the throne, in the
midst of the throng; with Christ high above the heavens,
low as an addict's hell-ridden shame. The variations in his
earthly latitude and longitude are numberless; but if you
take a reading by the Sun you will find his position to be
the place of a skull.

He knows his place. It is with the Great High Priest,
standing in the holy of holies in leather shoes or stiletto
heels to minister on behalf of the world. But even to
know this has its perils, Joe, and writing these letters I
have suddenly become afraid lest I do little else but make
you more aware of yourself. Self-consciousness is not a
sin, but it is the undiluted juice of the fruit of the tree of
knowledge—and easily goes sour. A Roman Catholic
priest, summarizing the plans of the Vatican Council in

regard to the laity, said that the first thing to do was to turn the layman in on himself so that he could understand himself and his dignity. The second thing was to draw him into the worship, 'the vital beating heart', of the Church—and for this reason worship must be contemporary. The third thing was to turn him out into the world, to be the 'apostolate', consecrated to consecrate the world. The Spirit is saying very similar things to the Churches! But note the phrase 'to turn the layman in on himself'. This seems to be an essential part of the process. St Matthew chapter 25 records the remarkable story of persons who had shown practical kindness to others, and who in the day of judgment could say 'When did we see You hungry?' Their concern for others, without knowing its implications, was a splendid thing. But by telling that story Jesus made sure that His hearers could never be among those with a similar ignorance. Ever since then we have known that He is the emaciated foreign refugee and the person who cannot find lodgings. He has exposed us to the sanctity of the meek and the perils of Pharisaism with one short parable. It is our awful privilege to know His position and ours.

This is what Lent is about. David Stacey writes of this season, 'It is the antechamber of humiliation in which we try to shed the garments of formalism and insensitiveness and self-esteem that make us unfit for the feast to come. It is a time therefore for searching rather than finding.' Well, we have a search on our hands. But our danger is that we may emerge cool and calculating, over-serious about our 'position', tense with new effort, pre-occupied with our attempts to live up to our high calling; and finish up objectionable prigs incapable of spontaneous liking and loving.

So we must take a still closer look at the city saint. We shall find, I think, that although holiness is God-likeness, he takes himself as he finds himself; although holiness is God-belonging, he takes life as he finds it; that although holiness is God-usefulness, he takes other people as he finds them. And behind all this, the saint has learnt to take God as he finds Him.

33

Friday

First, the city saint takes himself as he finds himself. His priestly vocation is the backbone of his life, and when he does a good job at work, or gets something done in local politics, or presents accurate youth club accounts, or makes a hospital visit on behalf of the Church, he finds satisfaction in it. But that is different from self-esteem, from the Little Jack Horner attitude, and from the 'I'm all right eternally Jack' approach. If the reward for loving were simply nice feelings of self-approbation, it would be worse than a box of poisoned chocolates as a thank-you present; in fact, the reward for loving is more love.

The saint knows the spirit if not the substance of Article 14 of the Thirty-nine Articles: that there are no works of 'supererogation', that a man cannot do more for God 'than of bounden duty is required'. The highest position he can reach is the joint one of 'blessed of my Father' and 'unprofitable servant'.

Further, his very worldliness keeps him to size. Like the priests of old, and unlike Jesus the High Priest, he must seek forgiveness for himself as well as others. He will value the insight of the Orthodox Church in its stress on identification with a sinful world. He will remember how those who went to be the Church in East Harlem compared Christ's action with theirs: 'He humbled Himself. We can't. There is no lower place for us to go.'

Christ teaches him to hate his life; not to neglect it, nor to speak disparagingly of himself, but to feel a basic dissatisfaction and contempt that after all he has received he is so un-Christ-like. His humiliation is complete because he cannot even indulge in despair and self-mortification. Christ is always picking him up; always insisting on his utter dependence; always accepting him, knowing exactly what he is. So all he can do is to accept himself, and to let Christ keep him low, and to give thanks.

There is something 'of this world' in taking yourself as you are. Religions say strive, march, fight. Christ says, 'Be yourself and let Me look after things, and put you in your place'. Because the saint knows his place, his life is not a constant effort to get to it, to defend it, or to justify his standing on it. He knows he is not holy by exertion. He is given his status.

Our concentration on holiness in these letters, Joe, could turn you into a self-centred struggler or a self-despairing straggler. You may try to understand holiness, but you must not try to attain it in grim determination. If you do, you will not be at all 'nice to know'. I remember the comment of a keen observer, 'If only you Christian people could relax and enjoy life'. Because the saint is 'in God', he can be in everything, and take life as he finds it.

It was Bonhoeffer who saw the artificiality of trying to force oneself into a pattern and to control experience. He was put off by the unnaturalness of religious people, and found a healthier attitude in the world. So in a letter dated 21st July 1944, he writes of the 'worldliness' of Christianity. He does not mean the shallow this-worldliness 'of the enlightened, of the busy, the comfortable or the lascivious', but something more profound with a death

and resurrection in it. He speaks of a young pastor who
wanted to be a saint, and says that he himself thought he
could acquire faith by trying to live a holy life. But such a
self-conscious effort is distasteful: 'One must abandon
every attempt to make something of oneself, whether it
be a saint, a converted sinner, a churchman (the priestly
type, so-called), a righteous man or an unrighteous one,
a sick man or a healthy one. This is what I mean by
wordliness—taking life in one's stride, with all its duties
and problems, its successes and failures, its experience
and helplessness. It is in such a life that we throw ourselves utterly in the arms of God.'

And thirdly, the city saint shows a worldly rather than
a pious slant by taking other people as he finds them.
His position as (in some sense) 'a priestly type' could
make it very difficult for him to meet another person
simply as a person, and not as a sinner, or a potential
saint, or a possible new member, or a useful contact, or
someone to serve.

To accept a priestly calling is to get rid of a great
deal of the irrelevancies of church life; but it is also to
occupy a privileged position. More and more today the
Church talks about service. Good—so long as we realize
the position we put 'the world' in by wanting to serve it.
It is hard for the Church, especially the western Churches,
to appreciate how uncomfortable it often is to be at the
receiving end. The very fact of giving puts one, or so it
seems, in a superior position. The old age pensioner, who
goes next door rice pudding in hand, has got hold of more
than a pudding when she says, 'Now dear, I hope you
won't be offended.' The truth is that giving without
love is always an insult.

At a Bible study group we were looking at the picture
of the perfect city in Revelation chapter 21. A youth

leader expressed considerable doubts about it. Would life be tolerable, let alone perfectly happy, in a community where nobody needed food or comfort? Would not love itself get lost? We decided that in the perfect city love is entirely mutual. Possessive interference, one-sided 'charity', unintended offence, dutiful kindness, all give way to the fulfilment of life in relationship, to the in-and-out of adventurous love.

The city saint lives already in this spirit. Every person is a new discovery, and he never gives without receiving. He recognizes that the bearing of a helpless invalid can be salt that savours a whole lump of living. He knows that God calls Cyrus 'my anointed' and the chairman of the humanist society 'my servant'. He will be glad that the laughter of children's voices in the playground makes a contribution to the city's life. And he will quietly accept his place in a world that is God's, grateful to know that he may be of most use when he is least conscious of himself and his calling.

34

Saturday

P.S. I said that the city saint has learnt to take God as he finds Him. Perhaps the best—the only—way to develop that thought is to make some attempt to discover what Christ is saying to him, through all his experiences. Could it be something like this?

This is My city, microcosm of My world.
Cities were built to house the gods. This city houses the aspirations of civilized men, the things they strive for and exalt, all they consider good and wise. Find Me in all these.
Cities were built for protection and peace. This city is

wide open to the attacks of bitter men and of tough
deprived youths, to the indulgences and deceits of accepted
existence, and to the threat of sky-borne destruction. Find
Me (you must look harder) in all these.

Where men and women work, and families relax together,
and children play and quarrel and make up, I am.

Where love is and hate is; where passion displaces common sense; where a wise word is spoken in jest; I am.

In board rooms and billiards rooms, My voice speaks
through men's voices, and is contradicted by men's
voices, and knows interference from men's voices.

Everywhere My Word is questioned, and My questions
are answered.

Everywhere My Law is unbreakable, and My laws are
broken. All serve Me. I serve all.

In this city I have a Body. It serves Me, in a kind of way.
Men are to see Me in its face, and experience Me in its
deeds.

I have other faces and other deeds. My Body is My
fullness. I have chosen and sent it. I build it up. In it
My judgment begins.

It represents to the city the unity of all mankind.

It represents to the city My love for any who might,
for any reason whatever, be regarded as the least
important of My brothers.

It is holy as I am holy.

So are you, within it.

I love you, not because you were baptized and brought up
with My name on your lips; not because you have made
some sort of response to My Word and Deed; not because
you have shown the slightest success in being like Me
or useful to Me.

I love you as a human being made for the Father.

I love you as you—a distinct moment in the full-scale symphony they call world history.

I love you because you live, as all men live, by the power of a Lamb slain from the foundation of the world.

As I love you, so I love all in the city. All are mine. And I am for all.

I am on your side. Never mind—at this moment—whose side you are on, or think you are on. I am on yours.

On your side and at your side.

In heaven, or in hell.

I have put you in your place. With me you will stand in heaven and alongside others. My place is in the holy of holies and the ungodly of ungodlies. You can come.

I have no resting place, no week-end cottage.

You have no place to lay your head—except My side.

Take the lowest place: that is where you belong.

You will find Me there.

Preparations for Holy Week

The Meditation for Holy Week that follows is based on the Readings for Palm Sunday, and especially on Zech 14^{20-1}. We shall be looking at Zechariah's vision of the perfected city of God and seeking the city saint in it. I set out here the main thought for each day:

Day 35: The city's religion is to be purified.

36: The city's religion is to be transformed.

37: Everything in the city is to be holy.

38: Everything is to be a holy sacrament to the city saint.

39: The city saint is to be a holy sacrament to everything.

40: The city saint is involved in a holy war.

Here is the list of Readings for Palm Sunday:

Zech 9⁹⁻¹⁰   The city's king
Zech 14¹⁻⁹, ¹⁶⁻²¹   City festival
Jn 7¹⁴⁻³⁹   Jesus at the festival
Mt 21¹⁻¹⁷   Jesus the city's king

The passage on which the Meditation is based is as follows (AV):

'In that day shall there be upon the bells of the horses, HOLINESS UNTO THE LORD; and the pots in the Lord's house shall be like the bowls before the altar. Yea, every pot in Jerusalem and in Judah shall be holiness unto the Lord of hosts: and all they that sacrifice shall come and take of them, and seethe therein: and in that day there shall be no more the Canaanite in the house of the Lord of hosts.'

Holy World

35

Monday

'no more the Canaanite'

Nowhere does the Bible refer to a holy world. The Psalmist comes near to doing so, when he sings of God Creator and Founder of all things:

'The earth is the Lord's, and the fulness thereof:
The world, and they that dwell therein.' (Ps 24¹)

But he immediately goes on to talk about one 'holy place' on which many in the world are unworthy to stand. Usually when Old and New Testament writers mention the world, they are thinking of a universe under evil influence, of a planet off-course, and of a fractious human race (Jn 3¹⁶, 14³⁰; Rom 3²³). God has a problem child.

Yet the prophets look to the day when 'all flesh' will worship God. That world is described by Isa 66²² as 'the new heavens and the new earth'. The Book of Revelation speaks of it as 'the holy city, new Jerusalem'. The historical career of Jerusalem has been as chequered as that of any city in the world, but St John the Divine follows a long line of Jewish prophets who fix their attention on Jerusalem as it will be when God completes His purposes for this age. For the (3rd or 2nd century) writer of Zechariah chapters 9–14, as for Ezekiel and others before him, the mediocre city points to the ideal community of 'that day'. In the Book of Revelation the 'holy city' symbolizes the holy world, given by God at the end— that is, the beginning—of all things.

At the centre of 'Zechariah's' city is the temple. He looks to the day when the religious life of the community will be utterly pure; the RV margin gives 'trafficker' for 'Canaanite' (14²¹). All sharp practice, all double-dealing, all unworthy acts will be 'no more'.

On this Monday of Holy Week we remember the time when Jesus turned out of the temple at Jerusalem its 'traffickers' (Mt 21¹²). Did some looking on see in this a sign that in the activity of Jesus the prophesied day had dawned? Is that why some were so angry; who did He think He was? Did others whisper, in the words Peter used later, 'this is that'? (Acts 2¹⁶).

The Protestant Reformation of the 16th century gathered momentum through the push of a hundred different protests against the corruption of the Church. In the end the inner courts of Church doctrine heard the whip of Luther's anger. In our day we hear whispers about the wealth under the Church Commissioners (a much misunderstood group); or the financial support that comes to churches from those who see nothing wrong with Bingo; or the individual clergyman who acts in an unprofessional manner. The general impression is that, compared with previous generations, the organized life of the Churches is outstandingly free from corruption. You might think that they were all fit to stand in the 'holy place'. It is the ineffectiveness of the Church that points the need for new reformation today.

But look again. How far is this ineffectiveness due to unholy—that is, un-God-like—elements in its life? We cannot (Letter 8) be the priestly people of God unless we

The prophet wants to see the whole world committed to
the paraphernalia of religious practices. Those who do
not respond, he confidently warns, will be punished with
drought—for the feast of tabernacles had to do with rain
for the crops. And he anticipates the retort from Egypt,
'Who cares; we have a river' by allocating a special
plague. George Adam Smith wrote of this passage years
ago:

'One is tempted to think what Amos or Jeremiah or
even "Malachi" would have thought of this. Verily
all the writers of the prophetic books do not stand upon
the same level of religion.'

There is no mention of the obedience of God through
justice and mercy. All is ceremonial and ritual—a grand
religious circus, horses with bells and the lot:

> Ride-a-cock horse to Calvary Cross,
> And see a fine lady ride on a white horse.
> Rings on her fingers, and bells on her toes—
> Her name is religion, and O what a pose.

We are reminded of the biting words of Kierkegaard a
century ago: 'We have what one might call a complete
inventory of churches, bells, organs, foot-warmers, alms-
boxes, hearses, etc. . . . and this is a peril, because it so
very easily gives rise to the misunderstanding that, having
such a complete Christian inventory, we naturally have
Christianity too.'

But it is not as bad as that in these days! Are you sure?
Many seem content that things should have a religious
tinge or fringe. We speak in missionary situations of
baptizing everything into Christ. This means taking the
traditional deeply-grained religious-social activities and
giving them a Christian content. But what does this
mean in our missionary situation? 'Abide with me' at

the cup final? Epilogues in youth clubs? Carols among
Christmas drunks? Prayer preceding everything?

And then dare to ask how religion-centred we are.
(Letters 9 and 10). How, for instance, did the impression
get around that the Christian is particularly, if not
exclusively, interested in getting other people to come to
church? When we do sally forth to forbidding doorsteps,
it is so much easier to talk about the church and its time-
table than about Christ and His; so much more congenial
to speak of our little realm than His Kingdom. We assess
our work by the size of our congregations, and define
revival in the same terms.

You may impatiently reply, 'Of course we hope our
"contacts" will link up with church affairs, and then see
the point of it all. Their best chance of finding Christ
is through this means.' But is it? Bonhoeffer's assertion,
which has struck like lightning, is that for multitudes
in the modern age religion is completely powerless to
bring them to Christ. Over four centuries our world has
turned into a secular world, in which people are out of
touch with, and indifferent or hostile towards, all organized religion. They will come to the truth of Christ
through secular things, or they will never come.

Those of us religiously 'well in' must note the ambiguity
of religious activities—that is, their power for evil or
good. Of course the modern protest against religion is
not modern. Amos, Hosea, Micah all spoke out against
hymns without justice and sacrifice without mercy.
Religion can burn up energy that should have been
devoted to the love of God in others; it can lead to hypocrisy; it can crucify Christ afresh. That is why, as a better
proposition than Christian religiosity, secular men speak
of religionless Christianity (Letter 6). Zech 14^{13} gives
us the hint that the city saint will have a double grip on

religion—with one hand holding on fast to it to wrest a blessing from it, and fighting it with the other.

Religion at its best is the 'carrier' of Christ. Perhaps we may take an analogy from St Matthew's story of Palm Sunday. Matthew, following the prophecy of Zech 9[9], says that there were two animals—an ass and her colt. The modern secular world is the child of religious Christendom. Jesus rides into His world using two mounts—religious and secular. For many people today He rides the colt, which is less motherly, friskier, not so predictable, but able to negotiate the road. If Bonhoeffer's prophecies come true, man-apart-from-religion will yet fling down his garments in the way.

Make everything religious! So we might understand 'Zechariah'. But that is just what the city saint must not do, for the holy God does not do it. His new Jerusalem has no temple in it; for 'in that day' Church and community are one, and the 'holy place' of God's presence is the world of people and things, and all life is like the spontaneous praise of children's voices.

37

Wednesday

'holiness unto the Lord'

It may be we were doing 'Zechariah' an injustice by focussing on his 'pots'. He also says that the bells on the horses will bear the inscription so far reserved for the high priest's mitre. Is there any other reference in the Old Testament that so clearly links the sacred and the secular? These are not the bells on the high-priests robe, indicating his aweful religious responsibilities, but the familiar accessories of every-day life.

Bells and holiness! We are encouraged to look again at the unexpected combinations, 'holy worldliness', 'worldly holiness'. Push aside for the moment the bad atmosphere conjured up by 'worldly', and ask how the word arises. In the Authorized Version it translates a Greek word (*kosmikos*) which in the writings of classical Greek is used of anything relating to the universe. At that stage there is no rebellious spirit in it whatsoever.

The word is only used twice in the New Testament. It comes at the beginning of Hebrews chapter 9, where the old covenant is compared with the new. The comment is made (AV) 'the first covenant had a worldly sanctuary', which RV gives as 'a sanctuary of this world'. This is surprising! Not only is there 'no prejudice' in the use of 'worldly' here—the comparison simply being between heaven and earth—but the reference is to a '*hagion kosmikon*', a worldly holy place!

The other reference brings us down to the earth, earthy. Titus 2¹² speaks of 'godless ways and worldly desires', and we noted earlier that once the world is seen as estranged from God 'worldly' gets into weak and rebellious company. The word is frequently used in this sense in early and later Christian writings and in modern conversation.

The 'Hebrews' use leads us to believe that the word 'worldly' is itself redeemable. We have seen that the word 'holiness' means God-ness, so we can never use the word 'holy' where we cannot think of God. And if 'worldly' is used to mean 'related to this world' that is exactly what we can do. The God who created the world for His glory, and delivered it from lostness by Incarnation, and works in men through the Holy Spirit—this God is, intricately and inextricably, related to this world. He is a worldly God. And holy worldliness is that sort of world-belonging-ness which is at the same time God-belonging-ness; while worldly holiness is that kind of God-ness which is in touch with the world as God is. What these cumbersome combinations are doing is encouraging us to adopt an attitude of mind that recognizes the world and all things in it as not only an enemy stronghold but the sphere of God's saving and sanctifying deeds.

Come a little further. The Latin version of the New Testament translated this word with 'saecularis'. Here we meet a familiar, though somewhat elusive, friend. 'Secular', too, simply means 'belonging to the world', and we may speak of God in another way—secular God, God active in all those realms of human life that no longer come under the control of the Church, God in the thick of the world's life, God of horses' bells as well as church bells.

And one more step. The New English Bible draws out the meaning of Heb 9^1 thus: 'a material sanctuary'. The world we speak of is a world of material things. And the God we worship in spirit is the God of material things, made for His use and blessing. The 'common' and 'profane' things—that is, things with no religious use— are His material.

We remember on this day of Holy Week the question asked of Jesus about payment of tax to a foreign, Roman, occupying power. The penny had Caesar's inscription, symbolizing the Roman civilization under which the Jews lived. 'Pay Caesar what is due to Caesar', said Jesus. (Mt 22$^{15-22}$). This cannot mean that there are realms where God's writ does not run. Jesus comment to Pilate is, 'You would have no authority at all over me, if it had not been granted you from above' (Jn 19^{11}). St Peter sees government as the secular servant of God, and after writing of the 'royal priesthood' of God's people he

recognizes the place of 'every human institution' (1 Pet
2¹³). The things of Caesar belong to God.

Yet all things are not yet subject to Christ-in-man (Heb
2⁹). God must reclaim lost ground. The horse, which
'Zechariah' sees in the new city, had been thought of
previously as foreign and unworthy (Zech 9¹⁰). And there
is the merchandise of Tyre! In Isa 23¹⁷⁻¹⁸ Tyre is
likened to a prostitute selling herself to every nationality.
Yet her ill-gotten gains are to become 'holiness to the
Lord'. The figure is startling, but the meaning is clear.
The goods of Tyre are to be devoted to the use of God's
people. That is what 'things' are for—to enrich human
life, to further human values. One day, 'Zechariah'
insists, all things will serve God's human race and (which
is the same thing) be holy to the Lord.

So we may paraphrase his words. Everything in the
world community is to have a God-stamp, a God-use, a
God-worthiness. 'IHS'—once embroidered on the pulpit
overhang—will be marked on every car horn and radio:
and coffee cups and glasses and camping-mugs and card-
board cartons will be valued like the communion set.
And the bell of the typewriter and the clang of moving
machinery and the referee's whistle and the diesel's
hoot will call men to the worship of a secular God. Life
itself takes on the dramatic splendour of high liturgical
worship.

38

Maundy Thursday

'all they that sacrifice'

The sacrifice was intended not only to be a representative
offering to God, but to convey God's cleansing and new

life to man. It was a 'mystery' which God used as a channel of help (Letter 5).

In the holy city everything brings God with it. All is His, His light is on all, and even the leaves of the tree are for healing (Rev 22$^{1-5}$). Everything is a 'sacrament', a 'mystery', a vehicle of God's gracious coming and a sign of His intimate Presence, a 'holy thing'.

In the modern city we know, not everything is available to God in this way; yet He turns even man's wrath to praise Him. Men partially insulated from the terrible electricity of the Holy One fail to recognize the 'signs' (Mt 16^3). And when the signs have made their impact, man goes idolatrous. St Paul affirms, 'His invisible attributes, that is to say His everlasting power and deity, have been visible, ever since the world began, to the eye of reason, in the things He has made' (Rom 1^{20} NEB). Yet, as Paul proceeds to show, in animistic life the things of nature have received the attention and respect due to the invisible God. And when man begins to make things, he makes an idol which, instead of being the symbol of his dependence and God-derived creativity, has become an end in itself.

In city life, things—the same things—can be related to men as idols, unworthy substitutes for the true God, or as sacraments, vehicles of His love. The late President Nehru called modern industrial plant 'the temples where men worship'. What do they worship?

God wills that city things shall be at His disposal, and Zech 14^{20} insists that humble, unexpected things, frivolous things, are His. The manufactured articles advertised on hoardings and telly, all that comes from the culture and creativity of modern civilization, the products of patient craftsmanship and the mass-produced, are all meant to be sacraments—not substitutes. There is a holiness of beauty as well as a beauty of holiness. And there is a holiness of the useful and the necessary. That the city saint may not forget this, he is given bread and wine.

On the occasion we commemorate this evening, Jesus took bread and wine and spoke of His Body and Blood, given for the world. In the worship of the Church on earth, other human hands perform the same actions, and other human lips speak the same words. In the ancient liturgies these material elements are held up with the words 'Holy things for the holy'. The Church of South India paraphrases, 'the things of God for the people of God'. The city saint receives his Lord not in natural elements but in prepared food. God and man together have produced the bread and the wine. Even these most holy tokens, says Pascal to his generation with stinging irony, can be a substitute instead of a sacrament:

'Christendom is a society of people who, with the help of a few sacraments, escape the desire to love God.'

The Society of Friends has taken the warning so much to heart that they will not risk the use of 'Sacraments' at all, making their very absence a constant declaration that all the things of the city and country are to bring God to men.

When we traced the correct meaning of holiness through the conventional meanings (Letter 2), we found four marks: ordinary appearance, separation, character, and inner power. The bread and the wine bear these marks. They seem ordinary enough. They are offered to God for a special purpose. They bear His character—the Body and Blood of the Lord—resembling Him in being material things offered as He offered Himself once for all. They convey His life, and speak of Him in us and us in Him.

Secular things too bear the same marks of holiness. They look 'common'. They are part of a world 'separated' from non-existence (we may say) for a holy purpose. They belong to a universe that bears the brand of its manufacturer—God-in-Christ. Within the life of city and world men are refreshed and invigorated by Him.

When Jesus was in Jerusalem for the feast of tabernacles He spoke strange words about going where His hearers could not find Him. They debated in their minds where He might be going. The most practical suggestion was that He was intending to go 'to the Dispersion among the Greeks and teach the Greeks' (Jn 7[32-6]). That would be to get lost. He would certainly be hidden there.

So it has come about. He is with all He has made and redeemed. Perhaps often we do not meet Him as we long to do because *we* have not 'dispersed' (Letter 9). In conversation with people far outside the chosen community, people of other religions and none, people of a secularized society, we may find Him. We shall share St Patrick's experience—'Christ in mouth of friend and stranger'. There will be many signs of His presence.

Everything is to be a holy sacrament to the city saint.

39

Good Friday

'living waters shall go out'

Today He was crucified. He suffered. The city put Him out; He overlooked the city. This is the Good Shepherd giving His life, knowing that His sheep will be scattered (Zech 13[7]; Mt 26[31]; Acts 8[4]). This is the Symbol of life, lifted up to draw all men to Himself (Num 21⁹; Jn 3¹⁴, 12³²). The city saint belongs to the Church of history, the Church under-trodden and over-treading, suffering and inflicting suffering, expanding and contracting, unshapely and reforming, dying and living. Today, worshipping a Suffering Servant, he learns again what it means to belong to a Servant Church.

How concerned and preoccupied are we about the influence of the Church in our generation? Is it this, rather than—as for Kierkegaard—the 'knight of faith', that 'occupies my thoughts exclusively'? We bemoaned in the letters (Letter 7) the weakness of the Church in city life. Does this mean we must conjure up new gimmicks, and ourselves 'rise up and make her great'?

Zechariah 14 is full of the longings of grandeur. The enemies of the Jews apparently scoffed at their dreams as delusions. Ezekiel took as the symbol of influence living waters flowing out of Jerusalem. But the only spring in Jerusalem, at the foot of Zion, finds its outlet in the Dead Sea to be lost for ever. So much for Jewish power! Yet 'Zechariah' takes Ezekiel's prophecy about power extending eastward to Asia, and says that from his new city another river will flow west. Not so long afterwards St Paul sailed from Seleucia (Acts 13⁴).

From the dead body of Jesus came water. John sees deep meaning in this 'healing stream', and seems to link it up with the waters of baptism which mark the extend-ings boundaries of the Church (Jn 19³⁴; 1 Jn 5⁶). The old Israel had dried up. 'Look', cries Jesus, 'there is your temple, forsaken by God.' (Mt 23³⁸ NEB) Today they shouted much the same at Him, as the temple of His body cried 'My God, why has Thou forsaken me'? (Mk 15³⁴). Yet from that death comes life to Church and world.

Jesus, who out of His holy, bloody agony cried, 'I thirst', had cried at the Feast of Tabernacles (Jn 7[37]): 'If anyone is thirsty let him come to me; whoever believes in me, let him drink. . . . Streams of living water shall flow out from within him.' The city saint has life to pass on—the life of the Spirit (verse 39). We are to think of holiness in moving, energizing, dynamic terms, bubbling up and out from the springs of our Rock.

'Zechariah' thinks of the influence of God's people in down-to-earth, 'worldly', warlike pictures. The nations will be conquered by force, and the survivors will worship in Jerusalem (14[16]). God's Church through the ages has had its bellyfull of war-conversions and power-politics, crusades and heresy hunts; not knowing what manner of spirit it is of. Jesus says to Peter, 'Put your sword in its sheath' (Lk 9[55]; Mt 26[52]).

Horses in Jerusalem are the symbol of power. We still speak of the capabilities of our largest engines in terms of horse-power. The Church is meant to move the world. It must find the appropriate weapons of its warfare, appropriate to its holy calling and character, appropriate today. Earl Haig wrote seven years after the end of World War I:

'Some enthusiasts today talk about the probability of the horse becoming extinct and prophesy that the aeroplane, the tank, and the motor-car will supersede the horse in future wars . . . I am sure that as time goes on you will find just as much use for the horse—the well-bred horse—as you have done in the past.'

How many think of the Church's power in just such a way. She will come into her own one day. It only needs a revival, on the lines of the past, to make her great, on the lines of the past. So long, of course, as her saints are well-bred!

We need new methods—but also a new humility and a new wonder at the resources at our disposal. The Church is the servant of mankind (Letter 10). Should modern church architecture compete with the multi-story offices, as Zech 14^{10} sees the earth a plain and Jerusalem lifted up to proclaim its spiritual pre-eminence? John Wesley's 'New Room' at Bristol, the first Methodist premises to be licensed for worship, is dwarfed by the giant confidence of great blocks of concrete and glass. Yet its plain modesty has something urgent to say. In that building Francis Asbury of the industrial Midlands volunteered for missionary service; and from it a river went out westwards to the new world. God comes to His world in unpretentious institutions and insignificant saints.

The city saint is to be a sacrament to everything. His life in the Spirit is to spread out in all directions, and mountains (Zech 14^{4}) will be removed in the process. The power of man over his material environment is immeasurably greater than in Zechariah's time—or fifteen years ago. He holds the diamonds, the uranium, and the planets in his hands. On behalf of mankind the cosmic saint will accept the power as God-intended and the responsibility as God-directed. His destiny is to share the Lordship of Christ. And as the world hovers between existence and extinction, wealth and poverty, fat paunches and empty breasts, he is poised as the priest of all things, the way through which God uses and serves His world.

This is an intolerable position, but so is the Cross intolerable, before which he remains humbled and held, bewildered and believing.

40

Holy Saturday

'the bells of the horses'

Jesus fulfilled the prophecy of Zech 9[9] when He rode into Jerusalem as the King of peace. He represents the God of peace who will ultimately reconcile all things in heaven and on earth (Col 1[20]) through Him. Yet He comes as a fighter, and He brings a sword (Mt 10[34], Eph 6[17]).

For 'Zechariah', writing of the city of peace, the presence of war-horses 'in that day' is the permanent reminder of warfare waged and won. The city has been bitterly engaged with God-opposing powers. Now all is victory and rest, but the tokens of war remain.

Today, Holy Saturday, it is as if He lies buried in the tomb; no one knows that He is vindicated by all the powers of heaven, that the crucial battle of human warare has been gloriously ended, that the loud cry 'It is accomplished' was a shout of triumph, that His self-commending 'into Thy hands' was the giving up of a life made perfect in sufferings, entirely sanctified, supremely successful.

Jesus in the flesh won the victory for all flesh. When He returned from His victory He bore the scars of battle. Still He says (Jn 20[27]), 'Reach your finger here: see my hands; Reach your hand here and put it into my side.' The witness of the apostles is (1 Jn 1[1]), 'We looked upon the Word of life and felt it with our own hands.' The greatest human privilege, given to St Paul (Gal 6[17]) and St Francis and every suffering Christian, will be to bear in the body the marks of Christ. The knight of faith 'has known the pain of forsaking everything in the world that was most dear to him'. The city saint gazes with rapture 'on those glorious scars'. The tokens of war remain.

His victory was over all that opposes God's holy love. In dying, says St Paul (Col 2¹⁵), 'He discarded the cosmic powers and authorities like a garment; he made a public spectacle of them and led them as captives in His triumphal procession'. Dr J. B. Lightfoot paraphrased this: 'As a mighty conqueror He displayed these His fallen enemies to an astonished world, leading them in triumph on His cross.'

He rode His cross like a war-horse.

All the bells of heaven and earth were silent then. Tomorrow morning early they will peal out, drowning all our sorrows. The Lord is risen. The world, and even the Church as we know it, are subject to Him.

But 'that day' of complete victory is yet to dawn, the day when He has abolished 'every kind of dominion, authority, and power'. What are the powers to be won over?—All the structures of modern life that militate against the advent of the perfect world community and the universal praise of God. And human lives, wills and emotions which at the deepest levels oppose and disobey the law of love. Structures and personalities have often been changed, through revolution and various forms of brain-washing. He turns the world upside down and gives new birth.

The city saint looks to that day. He waits for it. He sees the signs of it. His city life points in a thousand particulars to the city that has foundations. He belongs to that future, and serves it. For him the war-horses in 'Zechariah's' Jerusalem speak of the holy war, and their bells of ultimate victory.

St John the Divine has his own vision of those war-horses (Rev 19[11-16]). In it diadems are for victory, fine linen for 'the righteous deeds of the saints', and white for holiness. This is how he pictures the Lamb of God:

'Then I saw heaven wide open, and there before me was a white horse; and its rider's name was Faithful and True, for he is just in judgment and just in war. His eyes flamed like fire, and on his head were many diadems. Written upon him was a name known to none but himself, and he was robed in a garment drenched in blood. He was called the Word of God, and the armies of heaven followed him on white horses, clothed in fine linen, clean and shining.

'From his mouth there went a sharp sword with which to smite the nations; for he it is who shall rule them with an iron rod, and tread the winepress of the wrath and retribution of God the sovereign Lord. And on his robe and on his leg there was written the name: King of kings and Lord of lords.'

The eyes of the city saint never move from this flaming warrior who, on the Godward side of all experience and all created things, rides to victory. The saint will hesitate to cry for his bow of burning gold and his arrows of desire. His bow is tarnished, his arrows blunt. The warfare is being waged in him too. It is not in his power to build Jerusalem the holy city. Yet he, 20th-century secular man, is to share the holy worldliness of Him who rides through the world with singleminded passion and sacrifice. Let him be content, then, to be a bell on the Lord's war-horse. His strident jangling may wake others to the Word of God, riding to His triumph over all things. And the sovereign Lord Himself will write his inscription:

'Holiness unto the Lord'.

'Come, and maintain Thy righteous cause,
   And let Thy glorious toil succeed;
Dispread the victory of Thy Cross,
   Ride on, and prosper in Thy deed;
Through earth triumphantly ride on,
   And reign in every heart alone.'